Joana Robbins

BREAD MACHINE

COOKBOOK

HOMEMADE BREAD
IS EASY TO MAKE

240 RECIPES FOR
EVERY DAY

BREAKFAST BREADS

BREAD PERFECT FOR DINNER

Introduction

Hi!

My name is joana Robbins, and I want to share my long-time passion for baking bread with you. Ever since I was a young woman, I have always strived to create the perfect loaf. The smell of freshly baked bread filling the house has always brought me joy and comfort. Over the years, my collection of recipes has grown, enriched with new discoveries and time-tested secrets.

Now that I'm retired and have decades of experience under my belt, I decided to compile all my favorite recipes in this book. For me, bread is not just food. It is a symbol of warmth, care, and creativity. Each recipe in this book is a part of my life, a memory of wonderful moments spent in the kitchen, experiments, and small victories.

This book is not just a collection of recipes. It is my journey, my legacy that I want to pass on to you. Here, you will find recipes for every taste and skill level: from simple ones that even a novice baker can easily master to more complex ones that require patience and care.

Each recipe comes with detailed instructions and tips to help you avoid mistakes and achieve the best results. But most importantly, this book will help you experience the magic of turning simple ingredients into something amazing and tasty, such as Italian olive and rosemary bread, honey nut bread, and others.

Make your own bread according to your preferences, and don't worry if it turns out to be a funny shape or rises too much—it will still be an incredibly tasty piece of art.

Let this book become your reliable companion on the path to creating the perfect homemade bread. Join me on this exciting journey, and together we will create many wonderful moments in the kitchen.

Don't put it off until later—start your bread story today!

What's good about a bread machine?

Here are a few reasons why I love the bread machine:

The ease of use of a bread machine is remarkable! They usually have a simple and intuitive interface, making bread baking accessible even to beginners.

You have complete control over the quality and types of ingredients, which is especially important for health-conscious individuals or those with dietary restrictions.

You don't have to spend a lot of time baking; the bread machine does it for you.

The smell of freshly baked bread filling your home creates a cozy and comfortable atmosphere.

There are a variety of bread machine recipes that allow you to experiment with different types of bread, toppings, and ingredients.

Despite the greater automation of the process, there is still a lot of room for creativity. You can modify your favorite recipes and create new bread recipes exclusively for yourself or your family.

If you are an experienced baker, you likely know this. However, if you are just starting your journey into baking, you should know that the main ingredients for making bread in a bread machine usually include:

- Flour: The main ingredient for making dough. Wheat flour is commonly used, but you can also experiment with other types of flour, such as rye or oat.
- Yeast: To raise the dough. It can be fresh or dry, depending on the recipe.
- Water: For kneading dough and activating yeast.
- Sugar: Added to feed the yeast and maintain the sweet taste of the bread.
- Salt: To enhance flavor and regulate fermentation.
- Eggs: Provide protein, flavor, color, and a tender crust.
- Butter or vegetable oil: To soften the bread and improve its freshness.

Depending on the particular recipe or your tastes, you may add extra ingredients like milk, nuts, seeds, fruits, and more. It's vital to remember that not all breads require eggs, and you can modify recipes according to your particular dietary needs or preferences.

The following are the primary steps involved in baking bread in a bread machine:

- Measure the components first, then add the necessary ingredients (flour, water, salt, sugar, and yeast) according to the instructions.
- Next, load the bread machine, which entails adding the measured ingredients to its designated container.
- Choose the appropriate baking program based on the type of bread you wish to bake (e.g., French, white, rye, etc.).
- Setting the parameters correctly is crucial; adjust dough weight, crispiness of the crust, and other factors based on the recipe or your personal preferences.
- Start the program by pressing the "Start" button. During this time, the bread machine kneads the dough and bakes it.
- After the baking cycle is complete, the bread maker can also engage in a cooling step to prevent excess moisture and ensure the bread is easy to slice.

Each bread machine model may have its own unique features and parameters, but these steps represent the general process of making bread in a bread machine.

To facilitate comprehension, the bread-baking process can be separated into several phases:

- Combine and let sit: Before kneading, the ingredients are well combined and left to rest.
- Kneading: It's important to fully knead the dough at this point. It undergoes compression, twisting, stretching, and softening. Depending on the system and its settings, the full operation takes around thirty minutes.
- The initial rise: In this phase, the yeast converts sugar into carbon dioxide, which gives the dough structure, and alcohol, which gives it flavor – gluten.
- Blending: Before the second and third rise, the loaf is lowered, and the dough is uniformly distributed by the rotating blades of the bread machine.
- Second and third rising: The loaf will nearly double in size by the conclusion of the third rise, which takes around fifteen minutes.
- Baking: The bread forms into a completed loaf within the first five minutes of baking because the yeast in the dough is encouraged to thrive. The size, type, and level of baking of the loaf determine the baking temperature and time.

Cycles and settings

Most bread makers have similar cycles and settings:

- **Basic/White**: This mode is the standard for making yeast bread using white flour with a bit of whole wheat or oat flour added. This versatile cycle ensures perfect toasting.

- **Quick/Speed**: Used for recipes that require minimal time. Here, the rise time is shortened, and sometimes just one rise is done.

- **Sweet**: This mode involves a lower baking temperature and is intended for yeast bread with higher sugar, honey, or dried fruit content, giving a unique flavor and texture.

- **Whole Grain**: This cycle provides longer rise times for whole wheat or whole grain bread, which is especially important for forming gluten structure.

- **French**: This longer cycle is designed to achieve the gorgeous hard crust characteristic of European-style bread.

- **Quick Bread**: This cycle is designed to make yeast-free bread in just 2 hours, perfect for those who appreciate speed.

- **Jam**: This convenient cycle provides high heat while the jam is cooking. It is essential to be careful when removing the tray.

- **Dough**: If you prefer to bake bread in a conventional oven, this mode will help you prepare dough without kneading and kneading.

- **Gluten Free**: This cycle is designed to make bread with gluten-free flour, reducing the rise time compared to other cycles.

- **Other/Customization**: This can include various options such as increasing the baking or rising time, preset baking time, and other functions described in the manual.

Conversion table

Flour	
Quantity/Volume	**Flour weight (g)**
1 cup	120
3/4 cup	90
2/3 cup	80
1/2 cup	60
1/3 cup	40
1/4 cup	30
1 tablespoon	15
1 teaspoon	5

Sugar	
Quantity/Volume	**Weight of sugar (g)**
1 cup	200
3/4 cup	150
2/3 cup	133.33
1/2 cup	100
1/3 cup	66.67
1/4 cup	50
1 tablespoon	12.5
1 teaspoon	4.17

Oil	
Quantity/Volume	**Oil weight (g)**
1 cup	240
3/4 cup	180
2/3 cup	160

1/2 cup	120
1/3 cup	80
1/4 cup	60
1 tablespoon	15
1 teaspoon	5
Milk	
Quantity/Volume	**Milk volume (ml)**
1 cup	240
3/4 cup	180
2/3 cup	160
1/2 cup	120
1/3 cup	80
1/4 cup	60
1 tablespoon	15
1 teaspoon	5

Basic Breads

Mustard-flavoured General Bread

	Ingredients	Nutrition
2-Pound Loaf	• 1¼ cups milk • 3¼ tablespoons sunflower milk • 3¼ tablespoons sour cream • 2¼ tablespoons dry mustard • 1 whole egg, beaten • ½ sachet sugar vanilla • 4 cups flour • 1 teaspoon dry yeast • 2¼ tablespoons sugar • 2¼ teaspoons salt	• Calories: 340 • Fat: 5 g • Carbs: 54 g • Protein: 5 g • Fiber: 1 g • Sodium: 480 mg

Directions:

1. Remove the bread maker's pan and add the milk and sunflower oil, stirring them together. Then add the sour cream and beaten egg, mixing well.
2. Add the flour, salt, sugar, mustard powder, and vanilla sugar, mixing thoroughly.
3. Make a small well in the flour and sprinkle in the yeast.
4. Place the pan back into the bread maker and close the lid securely.
5. Select the "Basic" or "White Bread" setting and choose a medium crust.
6. Press the START button to begin the cycle.
7. Allow the bread maker to complete the cycle.
8. Once the cycle is finished, remove the pan from the machine and let the bread cool for 5 minutes.

Gluten-Free Bread

	Ingredients	Nutrition
1-Pound Loaf	• 2 cups rice flour, Potato starch • 1½ cups Tapioca flour • ½ cup Xanthan gum • 2⅓ teaspoon 2/3 cup powdered milk or ½ non-dairy substitute • 1⅓ teaspoon salt • 3¼ tablespoons sugar • 1 2/3 cups lukewarm water • 1⅓ tablespoons dry yeast, granules • 4 tablespoons butter, melted or margarine • 1 teaspoon vinegar • 3 eggs, room temperature	• Calories: 226 • Fat: 3 g • Carbohydrates: 29 g • Protein: 3 g • Sodium: 360 mg

Directions:

1. Begin by adding yeast to the bread pan.
2. Next, add all the flours, Xanthan/gum, milk powder, salt, and sugar to the bread pan.
3. In a separate bowl, beat the eggs. Mix them with water, melted butter, and vinegar.
4. Pour the egg mixture into the bread pan with the dry ingredients.
5. Select the "White Bread" setting on your bread machine with a medium crust setting.
6. Alternatively, you can choose a 3-4 hour cycle.
7. Start the bread machine and let it complete the cycle.

All-Purpose White Bread

	Ingredients	Nutrition
1-Pound Loaf	• ¾ cup water • one tablespoon melted butter cooled • one tablespoon sugar • ¾ teaspoon salt • 2¼ tablespoons skim milk powder • 2 cups white bread flour • ¾ teaspoon instant yeast	• Calories: 176 • Fat: 3 g • Carbohydrates: 27 g • Protein: 44 g • Fiber: 3 g • Sodium: 180 mg

Directions:

1. Begin by carefully adding all the specified ingredients to the bread machine according to the manufacturer's instructions.
2. Select the "Basic" or "White Bread" program on your bread machine and set the crust type to Medium.
3. Press the START button to initiate the bread-making process.
4. Allow the machine to complete the entire cycle.
5. After the bread is done baking, remove the bread pan from the machine and let the loaf cool for 5 minutes inside the pan.
6. Gently shake the pan to loosen the bread, then transfer the loaf to a cooling rack.
7. Once cooled, slice the bread and serve.

Anadama Bread

	Ingredients	Nutrition
2-Pound Loaf	• ½ cup sunflower seeds • 2¼ teaspoons bread machine yeast • 4½ cups bread flour • ¾ cup yellow cornmeal • 2¼ tablespoons unsalted butter, cubed • 1⅓ teaspoon salt • ¼ cup dry skim milk powder • ¼ cup molasses • 1½ cups water, with a temperature of 1 to 90 ⁰ F	• Calories: 180 • Carbohydrates: 25 g • Total Fat: 3 g • Protein: 3 g • Sodium: 360 mg

Directions:

1. Add the water, molasses, milk, salt, butter, cornmeal, flour, and yeast to the bread pan, excluding the sunflower seeds.
2. Place the bread pan securely into the bread machine and close the lid.
3. If your bread machine is equipped with a fruit and nut dispenser, add the sunflower seeds into it.
4. Turn on the bread machine and select the "Basic" setting, adjusting the crust color according to your preference. Then, press the start button to initiate the baking process.

Apricot Oat

	Ingredients	Nutrition
1-Pound Loaf	• 4 cups bread flour • 2/3 cup rolled oats • one tablespoon white sugar • 2¼ teaspoons active dry yeast • 1⅓ teaspoon salt • 1 teaspoon ground cinnamon • 2¼ tablespoons butter cut up • 1 2/3 cups orange juice • ½ cup diced dried apricots • 2¼ tablespoons honey, warmed	• Calories: 180 • Carbohydrates: 14 g • Cholesterol: 5 mg • Total Fat: 2.3 g • Protein: 1.3 g • Sodium: 360 mg

Directions:

1. Begin by carefully layering the bread ingredients into the bread machine's pan, following the recommended order provided by the manufacturer. Ensure each ingredient is added accurately.
2. As the knead cycle progresses, add the dried apricots into the bread machine's pan.
3. Once the baking cycle is complete, promptly remove the bread from the machine.
4. Warm honey slightly and then generously glaze the freshly baked bread.
5. Allow the bread to cool completely before slicing and serving.

Buttermilk White Bread

	Ingredients	Nutrition
1 ½-Pound Loaf	• 1½ cups water • 3 teaspoons honey • one tablespoon margarine • 1⅓ teaspoon salt • 3 cups bread flour • 2¼ teaspoons active dry yeast • 4 teaspoons powdered buttermilk	• Calories: 230 • Carbohydrate: 5.7 g • Cholesterol: 1 mg • Total Fat: 1 g • Sodium: 360 mg • Protein: 1 g •

Directions:

1. Begin by carefully layering the ingredients into the bread machine's pan, following the order recommended by the manufacturer.
2. Choose the medium crust and white bread settings on the bread machine.
3. Adjust the quantity of yeast based on the ambient temperature and humidity, using a few extra yeast granules during hot and humid summer months.

Homemade Wonderful Bread

	Ingredients	Nutrition
1-Pound Loaf	• 2⅓ teaspoon active dry yeast • ¼ cup warm water • one tablespoon white sugar • 4 cups all-purpose flour • ¼ cup dry potato flakes • ¼ cup dry milk powder • 2¼ teaspoons salt • ¼ cup white sugar • 2¼ tablespoons margarine • 1 cup of warm water (40° C)	• Calories: 180 • Carbohydrate: 31 g • Cholesterol: < 1 mg • Total Fat: 1.1 1/3 g • Protein: 4.5 g • Sodium: 480 mg •

Directions:

1. Start by activating the yeast in 1/3 cup of warm water mixed with sugar. Allow it to sit for 12-15 minutes until foamy.
2. Combine all the ingredients, including the activated yeast mixture, in the bread machine's pan following the manufacturer's recommended order.
3. Select the "Basic" setting and choose a light crust option on the bread machine.

Honey White Bread

	Ingredients	Nutrition
1-Pound Loaf	• 1 cup milk • 3¼ tablespoons unsalted butter, melted • 2¼ tablespoons honey • 3 cups bread flour • ¾ teaspoon salt • ¾ teaspoon vitamin c powder • ¾ teaspoon ground ginger • 1⅓ teaspoon active dry yeast	• Calories: 172 • Carbohydrates: 18 g • Cholesterol: 9 mg • Fat: 3.9 g • Protein: 5 g • Sodium: 180 mg

Directions:

1. Start by activating the yeast in ¼ cup of warm water mixed with sugar. Allow it to sit for 15 minutes until foamy.
2. Combine all the ingredients, including the activated yeast mixture, in the bread machine's pan following the manufacturer's recommended order.
3. Select the "Basic" setting and choose a light crust option on the bread machine.

Classic White Bread

	Ingredients	Nutrition
1½-Pound Loaf	<ul><li>½ cup (15ml) lukewarm whole milk</li><li>1 cup (25ml) lukewarm water</li><li>2¼ tablespoons white sugar</li><li>one tablespoon butter, melted</li><li>1 teaspoon. salt</li><li>3½ cups (400 g) wheat flour</li><li>2¼ tablespoons bread machine yeast</li></ul>	<ul><li>Calories: 180</li><li>Total Fat: 2.2 g</li><li>Sat Fat: 1.3 gCholesterol: 5 g</li><li>Sodium: 155 mg</li><li>Carbohydrates: 46 g</li><li>Dietary Fiber: 2.1 g</li><li>Sugars: 3 g</li><li>Protein: 7.3 g</li></ul>

Directions:

1. Start by carefully measuring and placing all the dry and liquid ingredients in the bread pan according to your bread machine's instructions.
2. Ensure accurate measurement by using cups, measuring spoons, and kitchen scales.
3. Set the baking program to "Basic" and select a medium crust type.
4. Monitor the dough consistency, and if it's too wet, adjust the bread machine settings accordingly. Allow the dough to cool for five minutes after baking.
5. Gently shake the loaf out of the pan, using a spatula if needed.
6. Wrap the freshly baked bread in a kitchen towel and let it rest for an hour before slicing, or transfer it to a wire rack.

Coconut Bran Bread

	Ingredients	Nutrition
1-Pound Loaf	• 3¾ cups wheat bread machine / white flour • 1¾ cups bran meal • 1¼ cups cream • 1/3 cup coconut milk • 2¼ tablespoons liquid honey • 2¼ tablespoons vegetable oil • 2¼ teaspoons salt	• Total Fat: 1½ g • Saturated Fat: 4.3 g • Cholesterol: 7g • Sodium: 480 mg • Carbohydrate: 59.4 g • Dietary Fiber: 3.3 g • Total Sugars: 6.7 g • Protein:1 g •

Directions:

1. Combine all the dry and liquid ingredients in the bread pan, following closely the instructions provided by the bread machine.
2. Use precise measurements with a cup, measuring spoons, and kitchen scale for accuracy.
3. Choose the "MEDIUM" crust setting and set the baking program to "BASIC."
4. Monitor the dough consistency during the mixing process, adjusting the bread machine if needed. Allow the dough to cool for five minutes if it becomes too wet.
5. After baking, wrap the bread with a kitchen towel and let it rest for an hour. Alternatively, place it on a wire rack to cool.

Milk White Bread

	Ingredients	Nutrition
1½-Pound Loaf	• 1¼ cups lukewarm whole milk • 5¼ cups bread machine wheat flour • 2¼ tablespoons butter softened • 2¼ tablespoons bread machine yeast • one tablespoon white sugar • 2¼ teaspoons salt	• Calories: 192 • Total fat: 4.5 g • Saturated fat: 2.2 g • Cholesterol: 11g • Sodium: 480 mg • Carbohydrates: 66.4 g • Dietary Fiber: 2.2 g • Sugars: 3.4 g • Protein:1.1 g •

Directions:

1. Carefully add all the dry and liquid ingredients to the bread pan following the instructions provided by your bread machine.
2. Ensure precise measurements using a cup, measuring spoon, and kitchen scale for accuracy.
3. Select the "Basic" or primary baking program on your bread machine and choose a medium crust setting.
4. Monitor the dough consistency during mixing. If it becomes too wet, adjust the bread machine settings accordingly. Allow the dough to cool for five minutes if needed.
5. Once baked, gently shake the loaf out of the pan. Use a spatula if necessary to release any stuck parts.
6. Wrap the freshly baked bread in a kitchen towel and let it rest for an hour. Alternatively, place it on a wire rack to cool.

Sour cream wheat bread

	Ingredients	Nutrition
1½-Pound Loaf	• 1¼ cups lukewarm whole milk • 5¼ cups wheat bread machine flour • 2¼ tablespoons vegetable oil • 2¼ tablespoons sour cream • 2¼ teaspoons bread machine yeast • one tablespoon white sugar • 2¼ teaspoons kosher salt	• Calories: 344 • Total Fat: 4.9 g • Saturated Fat: 1.3 g • Cholesterol: 1 g • Sodium: 470 mg • Carbohydrates: 64.6 g • Dietary Fiber: 2.2 g • Total Sugars: 1.7 g • Protein:1 g •

Directions:
1. Add all the dry and liquid ingredients to the bread machine pan, following your bread machine's instructions.
2. Carefully measure the ingredients using measuring cups, spoons, and a kitchen scale.
3. Select the "BASIC" baking program and set the crust type to medium.
4. If the dough appears too wet, adjust the bread machine settings and allow it to cool for five minutes.
5. Once the dough is thoroughly mixed, spread sour cream over the surface.
6. When the baking program ends, remove the pan from the bread machine and let it cool for five minutes.
7. Carefully shake the bread out of the pan, using a spatula if necessary.
8. Wrap the bread in a kitchen towel and let it rest for an hour, or cool it on a wire rack.

Vanilla Milk Bread

	Ingredients	Nutrition

2-Pound Loaf	• 4½ cups wheat bread machine flour
	
	• 1¾ cups lukewarm whole milk
	
	• one tablespoon white sugar
	
	• 1 packet vanilla sugar
	
	• 2¼ tablespoons extra-virgin olive oil
	
	• 2¼ teaspoons bread machine yeast
	
	• 2¼ teaspoons sea salt
		• Calories: 218
		
		• Total Fat: 5.7 g
		  Sat Fat: 1.4 g
		
		• Cholesterol: 4 g
		  Sodium: 480 mg
		
		• Carbs: 59.1 g Dietary Fiber: 2.1 g
		
		• Total Sugars: 4.6 g
		  Protein: 9.4 g

Directions:

1. Place all the dry and liquid ingredients into the bread machine pan according to the machine's instructions.
2. Measure ingredients precisely using a measuring cup, measuring spoon, and kitchen scales.
3. Set the bread machine to the "BASIC" baking program and select the "MEDIUM" crust option.
4. If the dough appears too wet, adjust the flour and liquid quantities accordingly.
5. Once the program ends, remove the pan from the bread machine and let it cool for five minutes.
6. Carefully shake the bread out of the pan, using a spatula if necessary.
7. Wrap the bread in a kitchen towel and let it rest for an hour, or place it on a wire rack to cool.

Country White Bread

	Ingredients	Nutrition
1-Pound Loaf	• 2¼ teaspoons active dry yeast • 1⅓ tablespoons sugar • 4 cups bread flour • 1⅓ teaspoon salt • 1 large egg • 1⅓ tablespoons butter • 1 cup warm milk, with a temperature of 15 to 115 °F	• Calories: 180 • Carbohydrates: 20 g • Total Fat: 4 g • Protein: 5 g •

Directions:

1. Start by placing all the liquid ingredients in the bread pan. Then, add all the dry ingredients except for the yeast.
2. Use your hand to form a hole in the middle of the dry ingredients and place the yeast in the hole.
3. Secure the pan in the bread machine chamber and close the lid. Choose the basic setting and your preferred crust color, then press start.
4. Once the cycle is complete, carefully transfer the freshly baked bread to a wire rack to cool.
5. Once cooled, slice the bread and enjoy!

Corn Bread

	Ingredients	Nutrition
1 -Pound Loaf	• 3½ cups corn flour • 1 cup water • 1½ cups bread machine wheat flour, sifted • 2¼ tablespoons butter softened • ½ cup cornflakes • one tablespoon white sugar • 2¼ teaspoons bread machine yeast • 2¼ teaspoons Kosher salt	• Calories: 319 • Total Fat 5.1 g • Sat Fat: 2.1 g • Cholesterol: 1½ g • Sodium: 464mg • Carbs: 62.3 g • Dietary Fiber: 4.11 g • Protein: 7.3 g • Sugars: 2.1 g •

Directions:

1. Place all the dry and liquid ingredients in the bread pan and follow the manufacturer's instructions.
2. Pay careful attention to measuring the ingredients accurately using the appropriate tools.
3. Set the baking program to Basic and select a medium crust setting.
4. If the dough appears too wet during mixing, adjust the flour and liquid quantities as needed.
5. Once the baking cycle completes, remove the bread from the pan and allow it to cool for five minutes.
6. Gently shake the loaf out of the pan and transfer it to a wire rack to cool completely.
7. Slice the bread and serve.

Cream hazelnut bread

	Ingredients	Nutrition
1 -Pound Loaf	<ul><li>3½ cups wheat bread machine flour</li><li>1 cup water</li><li>1¾ cups corn flour</li><li>5 ounces cream</li><li>2¼ tablespoons vegetable oil</li><li>2¼ teaspoons bread machine yeast</li><li>one tablespoons sugar</li><li>½ cup hazelnuts, ground</li><li>2¼ teaspoons sea salt</li></ul>	<ul><li>Calories: 405</li><li>Fat: 11 g</li><li>Cholesterol: 13 g</li><li>Sodium: 464 mg</li><li>Carbohydrates: 66.3 g</li><li>Fiber: 4 g</li></ul>

Directions:

1. Add all the dry and liquid ingredients to the bread pan following the bread machine's instructions.
2. Use precise measurements with a measuring cup, measuring spoon, and kitchen scales.
3. Set the baking program to "BASIC" and the crust type to "MEDIUM".
4. Adjust the flour and liquid quantities if needed to achieve the desired dough consistency.
5. After mixing, moisten the surface of the dough with water and sprinkle with hazelnuts.
6. When the program completes, remove the pan from the bread machine and let it cool for five minutes.
7. Shake the loaf out of the pan and transfer it to a wire rack.

8. Wrap the bread in a kitchen towel and let it rest for an hour before slicing and serving.

Cheese Breads

French Cheese Bread

	Ingredients	Nutrition
1½-Pound Loaf	1¼ teaspoon sugar 2⅓ teaspoons yeast 1¼ cups water 3 cups bread flour 2¼ tablespoons parmesan cheese 1 teaspoon garlic powder 1⅓ teaspoon salt	• Carbohydrates: 18 g • Fat: 6 g • Protein: 1½ g • Calories: 180 • Sodium: 230 mg

Directions:

1. Fill the bread maker with all the ingredients in the specified order and temperature settings recommended by the bread maker's manufacturer.
2. Close the cover, select the medium crust option for basic bread on your bread machine, and press the start button.
3. Once the bread has finished baking, remove it from the bread maker and place it on a cooling rack.

Beer Cheese Bread

	Ingredients	Nutrition
1½-Pound Loaf	• 1 package active dry yeast • 3 cups bread flour • one tablespoon sugar • 1⅓ teaspoon salt • one tablespoon room temperature butter • 1¼ cup room temperature beer • ½ cup shredded or diced American cheese • ½ cup shredded or diced Monterey jack cheese	• Calories: 180 • Carbohydrates: 18 g • Fat: 5 g • Protein: 5 g • Sodium: 360 mg

Directions:

1. Put the American cheese and beer in the microwave and heat them until they are barely warm.

2. Following the manufacturer's recommendations for temperature and sequence, add each ingredient to the bread machine.

3. Close the cover, select the medium crust setting for basic bread on your bread machine, and press the start button.

4. Once the bread has finished baking, remove it from the bread maker and place it on a cooling rack.

Jalapeno Cheese Bread

	Ingredients	Nutrition
1-Pound Loaf	• 3 cups bread flour • 1⅓ teaspoon active dry yeast • 1 cup water • 2¼ tablespoons sugar • 1 teaspoon salt • ½ cup shredded cheddar cheese • ¼ cup diced jalapeno peppers	• Calories: 185 • Carbohydrates: 23 g • Fat: 4 g • Protein: 7 g • Calories: 155 • Sodium: 290 mg

Directions:

1. Fill the bread maker with all the ingredients in the prescribed sequence and at the temperature suggested by the manufacturer.
2. Close the cover, select the medium crust option for basic bread on your bread machine, and press the start button.
3. Once the bread has finished baking, remove it from the bread maker and place it on a cooling rack.

Cheddar Cheese Bread

	Ingredients	Nutrition
1-Pound Loaf	• 1 cup lukewarm milk • 3 cups all-purpose flour • 1⅓ teaspoons salt • 1 teaspoon tabasco sauce, optional • ¼ cup Vermont cheese powder • one tablespoon sugar • 1 cup grated cheddar cheese, firmly packed • 1⅓ teaspoon instant yeast	• Calories: 182 • Carbohydrates: 25 g • Fat: 4 g • Protein: 7 g • Sodium: 300 mg

Directions:

1. Fill the bread maker with all the ingredients in the prescribed sequence and at the temperature suggested by the manufacturer.
2. Close the cover, select the medium crust option for basic bread on your bread machine, and press the start button.
3. Once the bread has finished baking, remove it from the bread maker and place it on a cooling rack.

Cottage Cheese and Chive Bread

	Ingredients	Nutrition
3-Pound Loaf	<ul><li>3½ cups water</li><li>1 cup cottage cheese</li><li>1 large egg</li><li>2¼ tablespoons butter</li><li>1⅓ teaspoon salt</li><li>3¾ cups white bread flour</li><li>3¼ tablespoons dried chives</li><li>2½ tablespoons granulated sugar</li><li>2⅓ teaspoons active dry yeast</li></ul>	<ul><li>Calories: 196</li><li>Carbohydrates: 33 g</li><li>Fat: 4 g</li><li>Protein: 7 g</li><li>Sodium 320</li></ul>

Directions:

1. Fill the bread maker with all the ingredients in the prescribed sequence and at the temperature suggested by the manufacturer.
2. Close the cover, select the medium crust option for basic bread on your bread machine, and press the start button.
3. Once the bread has finished baking, remove it from the bread maker and place it on a cooling rack.

Ricotta Bread

	Ingredients	Nutrition
1-Pound Loaf	• 3¼ tablespoons skim milk • ¼ cup water • 2/3cups ricotta cheese • 4 teaspoons unsalted butter, softened to room temperature • 1 large egg • 2¼ tablespoons granulated sugar • ½ teaspoon salt • 1½ cups bread flour, + more flour, as needed • 1 teaspoon active dry yeast	• Calories: 174 • Carbohydrates: 3 g • Fat: 1½ g • Protein: 11 g • Sodium: 120 mg

Directions:

1. Fill the bread maker with all the ingredients in the prescribed sequence and at the temperature suggested by the manufacturer.
2. Close the cover, select the medium crust option for basic bread on your bread machine, and press the start button.
3. Once the bread has finished baking, remove it from the bread maker and place it on a cooling rack.

Oregano Cheese Bread

	Ingredients	Nutrition
1-Pound Loaf	• 3 cups bread flour • 1 cup water • ½ cup freshly grated parmesan cheese • 3¼ tablespoons sugar • one tablespoon dried leaf oregano • 1⅓ tablespoons olive oil • 1 teaspoon salt • 2¼ teaspoons active dry yeast	• Calories: 184 • Carbohydrates: 23 g • Fat: 5 g • Protein: 3 g • Sodium: 230 mg

Directions:

1. Fill the bread maker with all the ingredients in the prescribed sequence and at the temperature suggested by the manufacturer.
2. Close the cover, select the medium crust option for basic bread on your bread machine, and press the start button.
3. Once the bread has finished baking, remove it from the bread maker and place it on a cooling rack.

Spinach and Feta Bread

	Ingredients	Nutrition
1-Pound Loaf	• 1 cup water • 2¼ teaspoons butter • 3 cups flour • 1¼ teaspoon sugar • 2¼ teaspoons instant minced onion • 1 teaspoon salt • 1⅓ teaspoons instant yeast • 1 cup crumbled feta • 1 cup chopped fresh spinach leaves	• Calories: 184 • Carbohydrates: 5 g • Fat: 6 g • Protein: 6 g • Sodium: 230 mg

Directions:

1. Fill the bread machine with all the ingredients (except the cheese and spinach) in the prescribed sequence and at the temperature suggested by the manufacturer.
2. Close the cover, select the medium crust option for basic bread on your bread machine, and press the start button.
3. Add the spinach and cheese with five minutes remaining in the last kneading cycle.
4. Once the bread has finished baking, remove it from the bread maker and place it on a cooling rack.

Italian Cheese Bread

	Ingredients	Nutrition
1½-Pound Loaf	• 1¼ cup water • 3 cups bread flour • ½ shredded pepper jack cheese • 2¼ teaspoons Italian seasoning • 2¼ tablespoons brown sugar • 1⅓ teaspoon salt • 2¼ teaspoons active dry yeast	• Calories: 180 • Carbohydrates: 1 g • Fat: 6 g • Protein: 7 g • Sodium: 350 mg

Directions:

1. Fill the bread maker with all the ingredients in the prescribed sequence and at the temperature suggested by the manufacturer.
2. Close the cover, select the medium crust option for basic bread on your bread machine, and press the start button.
3. Once the bread has finished baking, remove it from the bread maker and place it on a cooling rack.

Onion, Garlic, Cheese Bread

	Ingredients	Nutrition
1½-Pound Loaf	• 3¼ tablespoons dried minced onion • 3 cups bread flour • 2¼ teaspoons garlic powder • 2¼ teaspoons Active dry yeast • 2¼ tablespoons white sugar • 2¼ tablespoons margarine • 2¼ tablespoons dry milk powder • 1 cup shredded sharp cheddar cheese • 1½ cups warm water • 1⅓ teaspoon salt	• Total Fat: 6 g • Carbohydrates: 29 • Protein: 13 g • Sodium: 380 mg

Directions:

1. Fill the bread pan with the flour, water, powdered milk, butter or margarine, salt, and yeast, following the manufacturer's recommended order.

2. Select the basic cycle and medium crust setting on your bread machine. Add the shredded cheese, garlic powder, and two tablespoons of onion flakes when the machine signals with the sound alert.

3. Sprinkle the remaining onion flakes over the dough after the final kneading cycle.

Cream Cheese Bread

	Ingredients	Nutrition
1 Pound- Loaf	• ½ cup water • ½ cup cream cheese, softened • 2¼ tablespoons melted butter • 1 beaten egg • 4 tablespoons sugar • 1 teaspoon salt • 3 cups bread flour • 1⅓ teaspoon active dry yeast	• Carbohydrates: 24 g • Total fat: 4 g • Protein: 3 g • Sodium: 230 mg

Directions:

1. Arrange the ingredients in the bread machine pan according to the order recommended by the manufacturer.
2. After the cycle is complete, remove the dough from the bread machine and place it in a buttered 9 x 5 inch loaf pan.
3. Cover the pan and let the dough rise until it has doubled in size.
4. Bake at 350 degrees Fahrenheit for 30-35 minutes.

Mozzarella Cheese and Salami Loaf

	Ingredients	Nutrition
1-Pound Loaf	• ¾ cup water • 1/3 cup mozzarella cheese, shredded • 4 teaspoons sugar • 2/3 teaspoon salt • 2/3 teaspoon dried basil • Pinch of garlic powder • 2 cups + 2¼ tablespoons white bread flour • 1 teaspoon instant yeast • ½ cup hot salami, finely diced	• Calories: 184 • Carbohydrates: 23 g • Total Fat: 3 g • Protein: 6 g • Sugar: 3 g • Sodium: 350 mg

Directions:

1. In accordance with the manufacturer's Directions: , add all of the specified ingredients—apart from the salami—to your bread machine.
2. Select the Light crust type and Basic/White Bread program. Press "Start."
3. When the bread maker signals, add the remaining ingredients, including the salami.
4. Allow the bread machine to complete the baking cycle.
5. Once the cycle is finished, remove the pan from the bread machine and let it rest for five minutes.
6. Carefully shake the pan to remove the loaf, then place it on a cooling rack to cool before slicing.

Olive and Cheddar Loaf

	Ingredients	Nutrition
1-Pound Loaf	• 1 cup water, room temperature • 4 teaspoons sugar • ¾ teaspoon salt • 1 cup sharp cheddar cheese, shredded • 3 cups bread flour • 2¼ teaspoons active dry yeast • ¾ cup pimiento olives, drained and sliced	• Calories: 190 • Carbohydrates: 19 g • Total Fat: 4 g • Protein: 5 g • Sugar: 5 g • Sodium: 300 mg

Directions:

1. In accordance with the manufacturer's Directions: , add all of the specified ingredients—apart from the salami—to your bread machine.
2. Select the Light crust type and Basic/White Bread program. Press "Start."
3. When the bread maker signals, add the remaining ingredients, including the salami.
4. Allow the bread machine to complete the baking cycle.
5. Once the cycle is finished, remove the pan from the bread machine and let it rest for five minutes.
6. Carefully shake the pan to remove the loaf, then place it on a cooling rack to cool before slicing.

Green Cheese Bread

	Ingredients	Nutrition
1-Pound Loaf	• ¾ cup lukewarm water • one tablespoon sugar • 1 teaspoon kosher salt • 2¼ tablespoons green cheese • 1 cup of wheat bread machine flour • 5 cups whole-grain flour, finely ground • 1 teaspoon bread machine yeast • 1 teaspoon ground paprika	• Calories: 181 • Carbohydrates: 23.6 g • Cholesterol: 3 g • Total Fat: 1 g • Protein: 4.1 g • Sodium: 304 mg • Sugar: 1.6 g

Directions:

1. Fill the pan with all the liquid and dry ingredients (excluding paprika) and proceed according to your bread machine's Directions: .
2. Take extra care when weighing the components. To achieve this, use kitchen scales, a measuring spoon, and a measuring cup.
3. Use a saucepan to dissolve the yeast in the heated milk before adding it to the rest of the mixture.
4. After the buzzer sounds, add the paprika or put it in the bread machine's dispenser.
5. Select DARK for the crust type and BASIC for the baking program.
6. Adjust the amount of flour and liquid in the recipe if the dough is overly moist.
7. After the program is over, remove the pan from the bread maker and let it cool for five minutes.
8. Shake the pan to loosen the bread. When needed, use a spatula.
9. After wrapping the bread in a kitchen towel, leave it to cool for sixty minutes. Alternatively, a wire rack can be used for cooling it down.

Cheesy Chipotle Bread

	Ingredients	Nutrition
1-Pound Loaf	• 2/3cup water, 80°F • 1⅓ tablespoons sugar • 1⅓ tablespoons powdered skim milk • ¾ teaspoon salt • ½ teaspoon chipotle chili powder • 2 cups white bread flour • ½ cup (2 ounces) shredded sharp Cheddar cheese • ¾ teaspoon instant yeast	• Calories: 189 • Carbohydrates: 27 g • Total Fat: 1 g • Protein: 6 g • Sodium: 230 mg

Directions:

1. Fill your machine with the ingredients according to the Directions: .
2. Select a simple white bread program on the machine, choose Light or Medium crust, then press Start.
3. Take the pan out of the machine when the loaf is done.
4. Allow the loaf to cool for five minutes.
5. Remove the loaf by giving the pan a little shake, then place it on a rack to cool.

Cheddar Cheese Basil Bread

	Ingredients	Nutrition
1-Pound Loaf	• 2/3 cup milk, set at 80°F • 2¼ teaspoons melted butter, cooled • 2¼ teaspoons sugar • 2/3 teaspoon dried basil • ½ cup (2 ounces) shredded sharp Cheddar cheese • ½ teaspoon salt • 2 cups white bread flour • 1 teaspoon active dry yeast.	• Calories: 180 • Carbohydrates: 26 g • Total Fat: 4 g • Protein: 6 g • Sodium: 130 mg

Directions:

1. Fill your machine with the ingredients according to the Directions: .
2. Choose Light or Medium crust when selecting a program for the machine to make basic white bread, then press Start.
3. Take the pan out of the machine when the loaf is done.
4. Allow the loaf to cool for five minutes.
5. Remove the loaf by giving the pan a little shake, then place it on a rack to cool.

Double Cheese Bread

	Ingredients	Nutrition
1-Pound Loaf	• ¾ cup plus one tablespoon milk • 2¼ teaspoons butter, melted and cooled • 4 teaspoons sugar • 2/3 teaspoon salt • 1/3 teaspoon freshly ground black pepper • Pinch cayenne pepper • 1 cup (4 ounces) shredded aged sharp Cheddar cheese • 1/3 cup shredded or grated Parmesan cheese • 2 cups white bread flour • ¾ teaspoon instant yeast	• Calories: 183 • Carbohydrate: 18 g • Total Fat: 4 g • Protein: 6 g • Sodium: 244 mg

Directions:

1. Place all the ingredients into your device following its recommendations.
2. Select a program on the machine for basic white bread, choosing either a light or medium crust, and press Start.
3. Once the baking cycle is complete, remove the pan from the machine.
4. Allow the loaf to cool for 5 minutes.
5. Gently shake the pan, then remove the loaf and turn it out onto a rack to cool.

Chile Cheese Bacon Bread

	Ingredients	Nutrition
1-Pound Loaf	<ul><li>1/3 cup milk</li><li>1 teaspoon melted butter cooled</li><li>one tablespoon honey</li><li>1 teaspoon salt</li><li>1/3 cup chopped and drained green Chile</li><li>1/3 cup grated Cheddar cheese</li><li>1/3 cup chopped cooked bacon</li><li>2 cups white bread flour</li><li>11/3 teaspoons bread machine or instant yeast</li></ul>	<ul><li>Calories: 174</li><li>Carbohydrates: 40 g</li><li>Total Fat: 4 g</li><li>Protein: 6 g</li><li>Sodium: 230 mg</li></ul>

Directions:

1. Add the ingredients to your device following its recommendations.

2. Program the machine for basic white bread, selecting either a light or medium crust, and press Start.

3. Once the loaf is finished, take out the pan from the machine.

4. Allow the loaf to cool for 5 minutes.

5. Shake the pan gently to remove the loaf, then place it on a rack to cool.

Italian Parmesan Bread

	Ingredients	Nutrition
1-Pound Loaf	• 1/3 cup milk • 1 teaspoon melted butter cooled • one tablespoon honey • 1 teaspoon salt • 1/3 cup chopped and drained green Chile • 1/3 cup grated Cheddar cheese • 1/3 cup chopped cooked bacon • 2 cups white bread flour • 11/3 teaspoons bread machine or instant yeast	• Calories: 174 • Carbohydrates: 40 g • Total Fat: 4 g • Protein: 6 g • Sodium: 230 mg

Directions:

1. Add the ingredients to your device following its recommendations.

2. Set up a program on the machine for Basic White bread, selecting either a light or medium crust, and press Start.

3. Once it's finished, remove the pan from the machine.

4. Allow the loaf to cool for 5 minutes.

Feta Oregano Bread

	Ingredients	Nutrition
1-Pound Loaf	• 2/3 cup of milk, at 80°F • 2¼ teaspoons melted butter, cooled • 2¼ teaspoons sugar • 2/3 teaspoon salt • 2¼ teaspoons dried oregano • 2 cups white bread flour • 1⅓ teaspoon bread machine or instant yeast • 2/3 cup (2½ ounces) crumbled feta cheese	• Calories: 180 • Carbohydrates: 27 g • Fat: 4 g • Protein: 5 g • Sodium: 180 mg

Directions:

1. Add the ingredients to your device following its recommendations.

2. Program the machine for Basic White bread, selecting either a light or medium crust, and press Start.

3. Once it's finished, remove the pan from the machine.

4. Allow the loaf to cool for 3-5 minutes.

Breakfast Breads

English muffin

	Ingredients	Nutrition
1 Pound Loaf	<ul><li>1 teaspoon vinegar</li><li>1 cup water</li><li>1 cup lukewarm milk</li><li>2 tablespoons butter or 2 tablespoons vegetable oil</li><li>1½ teaspoons salt</li><li>1½ teaspoons sugar</li><li>½ teaspoon baking powder</li><li>3½ cups unbleached all-purpose flour</li><li>2 teaspoons instant yeast</li></ul>	<ul><li>Calories: 190</li><li>Carbohydrates: 13 g</li><li>Fat: 1.2 g</li><li>Protein: 2.2 g</li><li>Sodium: 360 mg</li></ul>

Directions:

1. Begin by adding the ingredients into your bread machine according to the specific guidelines for your model.

2. Secure the lid, select the basic bread setting with a light crust option, and start the baking process.

3. Once your bread machine signals that it has finished, remove the bread and transfer it to a cooling rack to cool.

Cranberry Orange Breakfast

	Ingredients	Nutrition
1½-Pound Loaf	<ul><li>1½ cups orange juice</li><li>2 tablespoons vegetable oil</li><li>2 tablespoons honey</li><li>3 cups bread flour</li><li>1½ tablespoon dry milk powder</li><li>½ teaspoon ground cinnamon</li><li>½ teaspoon ground allspice</li><li>1½ teaspoon salt</li><li>1 package active dry yeast</li><li>1¼ tablespoon grated orange zest</li><li>1 cup sweetened dried cranberries</li><li>1/3 cup chopped walnuts</li></ul>	<ul><li>Calories: 180</li><li>Carbohydrates: 29 g</li><li>Fat: 2 g</li><li>Protein: 9.1 g</li><li>Sodium: 246 mg</li></ul>

Directions:

1. Carefully add each ingredient to your bread maker according to the manufacturer's Directions: for order and temperature.
2. Secure the lid, set the machine to the basic bread setting with a light crust preference, and start the cycle.

3. A few minutes before the last kneading cycle completes, stir in the cranberries and chopped walnuts.

4. Once the bread is fully baked, remove it from the machine and allow it to cool on a cooling rack.

Buttermilk Honey

	Ingredients	Nutrition
1 Pound Loaf	<ul><li>½ cup water</li><li>¾ cup buttermilk</li><li>¼ cup honey</li><li>3 tablespoons butter, softened and cut into pieces</li><li>3 cups bread flour</li><li>1½ teaspoons salt</li><li>2 teaspoons yeast</li></ul>	<ul><li>Calories: 224</li><li>Carbohydrates: 19 g</li><li>Fat: 1 g</li><li>Protein: 2.2 g</li><li>Sodium: 362 mg</li></ul>

Directions:

1. Place each ingredient into the bread machine according to your manufacturer's specifications for order and temperature.

2. Close the cover, select the basic bread program with the medium crust setting, and start baking.

3. Once the bread is finished, carefully remove it from the machine and allow it to cool on a rack.

Whole Wheat Breakfast

	Ingredients	Nutrition
1½ - Pound Loaf	• 3 cups white whole wheat flour • ½ teaspoon salt • 1 cup water • ½ cup coconut oil, liquefied • 4 tablespoons honey • 2½ teaspoons active dry yeast	• Calories: 183 • Carbohydrates: 11 g • Fat: 3 g • Protein: 1 g • Sodium: 120 mg

Directions:

1. Load each ingredient into the bread machine according to the order and temperature settings specified in your manufacturer's guide.

2. Close the lid, select the basic bread setting with a medium crust, and press the start button.

3. Once the bread machine completes its cycle, remove the bread and place it on a cooling rack to cool.

Cinnamon-Raisin

	Ingredients	Nutrition
1½ Pound Loaf	<ul><li>1 cup water</li><li>2 tablespoons butter, softened</li><li>3 cups Gold Medal Better for Bread flour</li><li>3 tablespoons sugar</li><li>1½ teaspoons salt</li><li>1 teaspoon ground cinnamon</li><li>2¾ teaspoons bread machine yeast</li><li>¾ cup raisins</li></ul>	<ul><li>Calories: 181</li><li>Carbohydrates: 31 g</li><li>Fat: 2 g</li><li>Protein: 4 g</li><li>Sodium: 362 mg</li></ul>

Directions:

1. Place each ingredient, except the raisins, into the bread machine following the order and temperature recommendations from your manufacturer.
2. Close the lid, select either the sweet or basic bread setting with a medium crust, and start the machine.
3. Incorporate the raisins into the dough five minutes before the final kneading cycle finishes.
4. Once the bread is fully baked, carefully remove it and place it on a cooling rack.

Cranberry & Golden Raisin

	Ingredients	Nutrition
1½-Pound Loaf	• 11/3 cups water • 4 tablespoons sliced butter • 3 cups flour • 1 cup old fashioned oatmeal • 1/3 cup brown sugar • 1 teaspoon salt • 4 tablespoons dried cranberries • 4 tablespoons golden raisins • 2 teaspoons bread machine yeast	• Calories: 195 • Carbohydrates: 33 g • Fat: 3 g • Protein: 4.2 g • Sodium: 240 mg

Directions:

1. As directed by the manufacturer, load all of the ingredients—except for the cranberries and golden raisins—into the bread machine.
2. Secure the lid, select either the sweet or basic bread setting with a medium crust, and start the baking process.
3. Five minutes before the final kneading cycle ends, add the cranberries and golden raisins.
4. Once the bread has finished baking, carefully remove it from the machine and place it on a cooling rack.

Peanut Butter and Jelly

	Ingredients	Nutrition
1½-Pound Loaf	<ul><li>1½ tablespoons vegetable oil</li><li>1 cup of water</li><li>½ cup blackberry jelly</li><li>½ cup peanut butter</li><li>1½ teaspoon salt</li><li>1½ tablespoon white sugar</li><li>2 cups of bread flour</li><li>1 cup whole-wheat flour</li><li>1½ teaspoons active dry yeast</li></ul>	<ul><li>Calories: 192</li><li>Carbohydrates: 11 g</li><li>Fat: 9 g</li><li>Cholesterol: 0 mg</li><li>Protein: 4 g</li><li>Fiber: 2 g</li><li>Sugars: 11.2 g</li><li>Sodium: 244 mg</li><li>Potassium: 1 mg</li></ul>

Directions:

1. Load all ingredients into the bread machine pan.
2. Choose the basic program setting on your machine.
3. Press the start button to begin the baking process.
4. Once the baking is finished, remove the pan and let the bread rest for 5 minutes.

Bread perfect for Dinner

Corn Poppy Seeds Sour Cream Bread

	Ingredients	Nutrition
1½-Pounds Loaf	• 3½ cups all-purpose flour • 1¾ cups of corn flour • 5 ounces sour cream • 2¼ tablespoons corn oil • 2¼ teaspoons active dry yeast • 2¼ teaspoons salt • 5¼ ounces lukewarm water • poppy seeds for sprinkling •	• Calories: 223 • Total Fat: 4.1½ g • Saturated Fat: 1.6 g • Cholesterol: 4 g • Sodium: 297 mg • Carbohydrates: 39.9 g • Dietary Fiber: 2.6 g • Total Sugars: 0.3 g • Protein: 5.3 g • Vitamin D: 0 mcg • Calcium:1mg • Iron: 2 mg • Potassium: 117 mg •

Directions:

1. Choose "MEDIUM" for the crust color and set your bread maker's program to "BASIC".
2. Press the START button.
3. After kneading, sprinkle poppy seeds on top of the loaf and give it a quick spray of water.
4. Wait for the program to finish.
5. After it finishes, remove the bread pan and allow the loaf to cool for five minutes.
6. Shake the loaf out of the pan and place it on a cooling rack to cool for half an hour.
7. Cut, serve, and savor the aroma of freshly baked bread.

Oatmeal Bread

	Ingredients	Nutrition
1½-Pound Loaf	• 1⅓ teaspoon active dry yeast • 2 cups white bread flour, sifted • ½ cup • oatmeal flour • 1 teaspoon salt • 2¼ tablespoons liquid honey (can be replaced with sugar) • ½ cup • yogurt • one tablespoon butter, melted • ¾ cup • lukewarm water • 2¼ tablespoons oatmeal flakes	• Calories: 176 • Total Fat: 2.3 g • Saturated Fat: 1.3 g • Sodium: 230 mg • Carbohydrate: 32.9 g • Dietary Fiber: 1.6 g • Sugars: 5.5 g • Protein: 5.5 g •

Directions:

1. Gather all your bread ingredients and your measuring tools (cup, spoon, and kitchen scales).
2. Carefully measure and fill the pan with the ingredients.
3. According to the instructions on your bread machine, place all ingredients into the bread bucket in the correct order.
4. Close the lid.
5. Choose "MEDIUM" for the crust color and set your bread maker's program to "BASIC".

6. Press the START button.
7. Sprinkle oat flakes over the loaf and brush its surface with egg yolk or water after kneading.
8. Allow the program to complete.
9. Once finished, remove the bread pan and let it cool for five to ten minutes.
10. Carefully shake the loaf out of the pan and place it on a cooling rack to cool for half an hour.

Simple Dark Rye Bread

	Ingredients	Nutrition
1-Pound Loaf	• 2/3 cup lukewarm water • one tablespoon melted butter cooled • ¼ cup molasses • ⅓ teaspoon salt • one tablespoon unsweetened cocoa powder • ½ cup rye flour • pinch of ground nutmeg • 1¼ cups white wheat flour sifted • 1 teaspoon active dry yeast	• Calories: 181 • Total Fat: 2.1 g • Saturated Fat: 1 g • Cholesterol: 4 g • Sodium: 60 mg • Carbohydrates: 29.4 g • Dietary Fiber: 2.7g • Sugars: 6 g • Protein: 4.3 g • Vitamin D: 1 mcg • Calcium: 30 mg • Iron: 2 mg • Potassium: 241 mg

Directions:

1. Prepare all the bread components and assemble the measuring equipment (spoons, cups, and kitchen scales).

2. Carefully fill the bread machine pan with the ingredients.

3. Place all ingredients into the bread bucket in the sequence specified in your bread maker's handbook.

4. Close the lid.

5. Select the "MEDIUM" crust setting and choose the "BASIC" program on the bread maker.

6. Allow the program to complete.

7. After it finishes, remove the bread bucket and let it cool for five minutes.

8. Remove the bread from the pan and allow it to cool for 30 minutes on a rack.

Walnut Bread

	Ingredients	Nutrition
1-Pound Loaf	• 4 cups wheat flour, sifted • ½ cup lukewarm water • ½ cup lukewarm milk • 2 whole eggs • ½ cup walnuts, fried and chopped • one tablespoon walnut oil • one tablespoon brown sugar • 1 teaspoon salt • 1 teaspoon active dry yeast	• Calories: 257 • Total Fat: 6.7 g • Saturated Fat: 1 g • Cholesterol: 34 g • Sodium: 242 mg • Carbohydrate: 40.1 g • Dietary Fiber: 1.7 g • Sugars: 3 g • Protein:1.3 g •

Directions:

1. Gather all necessary ingredients for your bread, along with measuring tools (a cup, spoon, and kitchen scales).
2. Precisely measure each ingredient and add them to the bread pan.
3. Place all ingredients into the bread bucket in the correct order, as per your bread machine manual.
4. Close the lid of the bread machine.
5. Set your bread machine to the FRENCH BREAD program and select the MEDIUM crust color.
6. Press the START button.
7. Allow the program to complete its cycle.
8. Once the cycle is finished, remove the bread pan and let it cool for 5 minutes.
9. Turn the bread out from the pan and let it cool on a rack for 30 minutes.

Sauerkraut Bread

	Ingredients	Nutrition
1½-Pound Loaf	• 1 cup lukewarm water • ¼ cup cabbage brine • ½ cup finely chopped cabbage • 2¼ tablespoons sunflower oil • 2¼ teaspoons white sugar • 1⅓ teaspoon salt • 2 1/3 cups rye flour • 2 1/3 cups wheat flour • 2¼ teaspoons dry kvass • 2¼ teaspoons active dry yeast	• Calories: 297 • Total Fat: 4.9 g • Saturated Fat: 0.5 g • Cholesterol: 0 g • Sodium: 360 mg • Carbohydrates: 55.5 g • Dietary Fiber: 9.7 g • Sugars: 1.6 g • Protein: 9.5 g •

Directions:
1. Prepare all the ingredients for your bread and gather measuring tools (a cup, spoon, and kitchen scales).
2. Finely chop the sauerkraut.
3. Carefully measure and add the ingredients into the bread machine pan.
4. Place all the ingredients into the bread bucket in the specified order, following your bread machine manual.
5. Close the lid securely.
6. Set your bread machine to the "BASIC" program and choose the DARK crust option. Press START.
7. Allow the program to run its course.
8. When the cycle is complete, remove the bread pan and let it cool for 5 minutes.
9. Turn the bread out of the pan and let it cool on a wire rack for 30 minutes.

Rice Bread

	Ingredients	Nutrition
2-Pound Loaf	• 4½ cups all-purpose flour • 1 cup of rice, cooked • 1 cup water • 1 whole egg, beaten • 2¼ tablespoons of milk powder • 2¼ teaspoons active dry yeast • 2¼ tablespoons butter, melted • one tablespoon sugar • 2¼ teaspoons salt • 1¼ cups lukewarm water	• Calories: 197 • Total Fat: 2.1g • Saturated Fat: 1.1 g • Cholesterol:1 g • Sodium: 481 mg • Carbohydrates: 37.1 g • Dietary Fiber: 1.3 g • Sugars: 1.4 g • Protein: 5.6 g • Vitamin D: 2 mcg • Calcium: 23 mg • Iron: 2 mg • Potassium: 55 mg

Directions:
1. Gather all the necessary ingredients and measuring tools (cup, spoon, kitchen scales).
2. Carefully measure each ingredient and add them to the bread machine pan.
3. Place all ingredients into the bread bucket in the correct order, following your bread machine's manual.
4. Close the lid.
5. Set the bread machine to the "BASIC" program and select the crust color to "MEDIUM".
6. Press START.
7. Allow the program to run until it completes.
8. Once finished, remove the bread pan and let it cool for 5 minutes.

9. Remove the loaf from the pan and let it cool on a wire rack for 30 minutes.

Rice Wheat Bread

	Ingredients	Nutrition
2-Pound Loaf	• 4½ cups wheat bread flour • 1 cup water • 1 cup rice, cooked • 1 whole egg • 2¼ tablespoons soy sauce • 2¼ teaspoons active dried yeast • 2¼ tablespoons melted butter • one tablespoon brown sugar • 2¼ teaspoons kosher salt	• Calories: 318 • Total Fat: 4.3 g • Saturated Fat: 2.1 g • Cholesterol: 18 g • Sodium:407 mg • Carbohydrates: 60.4 g • Dietary Fiber: 2.3 g • Sugars: 1.4g • Protein: 9.1 g

Directions:

1. Gather your measuring supplies (cup, spoon, kitchen scales) and all the ingredients for your bread.
2. Carefully measure the ingredients into the bread pan.
3. Place every part in the correct order into the bread bucket. Consult the handbook for the bread maker.
4. Close the cover.
5. Set the crust color to "MEDIUM" on your bread maker and choose the "BASIC" program.
6. Press the START button.
7. Wait until the cycle is complete.
8. After finishing, remove the bread bucket and let it cool for five minutes.

9. Remove the bread from the pan and place it on a cooling rack to cool for thirty minutes.

Pepper Bread

	Ingredients	Nutrition
1-Pound Loaf	• ¾ cup + one tablespoon lukewarm milk • 3¼ tablespoons ground red pepper • 4 teaspoons fresh red pepper, chopped and roasted • 2¼ tablespoons butter, melted • 2¼ tablespoons brown sugar • 2/3 teaspoon salt • 2 cups wheat flour • 1 teaspoon active dry yeast	• Calories: 179 • Fat: 4.5 g • Cholesterol: 5 g • Sodium: 180 mg • Carbohydrates: 33 g • Fiber: 2.3 g • Sugar: 6.1 g • Protein: 5.1 g • Calcium: 40 mg •

Directions:

1. Gather all necessary ingredients and measuring tools (cup, spoon, kitchen scales).
2. Accurately measure and add the ingredients to the bread machine pan.
3. Follow your bread machine's instructions for placing the ingredients into the pan in the correct order.
4. Close the lid.
5. Set the bread machine to the "BASIC" program and select a "MEDIUM" crust.
6. Press the START button.

7. Allow the program to run until completion.
8. Once finished, remove the pan and let it cool for 5 minutes.
9. Turn out the loaf onto a cooling rack and let it cool for 30 minutes.

Sourdough Breads

Honey Sourdough Bread

	Ingredients	Nutrition
1 -Pound Loaf	• 2/3 cup sourdough starter • ½ cup water • one tablespoon vegetable oil • 2¼ tablespoons honey • ½ teaspoon salt • ½ cup high protein: wheat flour • 2 cups bread flour • 1 teaspoon active dry yeast	• Calories: 175 • Carbohydrates: 33 g • Total Fat: 0.3 g • Protein: 5.6 g • Fiber: 1.7 g • Sodium: 118 mg

Directions:

1. Pour the measured starter and all other bread ingredients into the pan of the bread machine.

2. Choose the "Basic" or "White Bread" setting with a light to medium crust option.

Czech Sourdough Bread

	Ingredients	Nutrition
1-Pound Loaf	• 1 cup non-dairy milk • one tablespoon salt • one tablespoon honey • 1 cup sourdough starter • 1½ cups rye flour • 1 cup bread flour • ¾ cup wheat flour • 1½ cup grated half-baked potato • 5 tablespoons wheat gluten • 2¼ teaspoons caraway seeds	• Calories: 191 • Carbohydrates: 39.9 g • Total Fat: 0.1½ g • Protein: 6.5 g • Sodium: 183 mg • Fiber: 4.3 g

Directions:

1. Combine all ingredients in the bread machine pan, following the recommended order specified by the machine's manual.

2. Select the "Dough" setting on the bread machine and start the cycle.

Sauerkraut Rye

	Ingredients	Nutrition
1-Pound Loaf	• 1 cup sauerkraut, rinsed and drained • ¾ cup warm water • 1⅓ tablespoons molasses • 1⅓ tablespoons butter • 1⅓ tablespoons brown sugar • 1 teaspoon caraway seeds • 1⅓ teaspoon salt • 1 cup rye flour • 2 cups bread flour • 1⅓ teaspoon active dry yeast	• Calories: 174 • Fat: 3 g • Carbohydrates: 11 g • Protein: 3 g • Sodium: 360 mg • Fiber: 1 g •

Directions:

1. Combine all ingredients into the bread machine pan in the order specified by the manufacturer.

2. Select the "Basic" or "White Bread" program on your bread machine and adjust the crust setting to "Medium."

3. Allow the bread machine to complete the cycle.

4. Once the cycle is finished, remove the bread pan from the machine and let the bread cool inside the pan for 5 minutes.

5. Carefully shake the bread pan to release the loaf, then transfer the bread to a wire rack to cool completely before slicing.

Pumpernickel Bread

	Ingredients	Nutrition
1½-Pound Loaf	• 1½ cups warm water • 1⅓ tablespoons vegetable oil • 1/3 cup molasses • 3¼ tablespoons cocoa • one tablespoon caraway seed (optional) • 1⅓ teaspoon salt • 1½ cups of bread flour • 1 cup of rye flour • 1 cup whole wheat flour • 1⅓ tablespoons of vital wheat gluten (optional) • 2⅓ teaspoon of bread machine yeast	• Calories: 197 • Fat: 1 g • Carbohydrates: 19 g • Sodium: 230 mg • Protein: 3 g •

Directions:

1. Start by adding all the ingredients into the bread machine pan.
2. Select the "Basic" bread cycle on your bread machine.
3. After the loaf has finished baking, move it to a wire rack and allow it to cool completely before slicing and serving.

Crusty Sourdough Bread

	Ingredients	Nutrition
1-Pound Loaf	• ½ cup water • 3 cups bread flour • 2¼ tablespoons sugar • 1⅓ teaspoon salt • 1 teaspoon bread machine or quick active dry yeast	• Calories: 155 • Carbohydrates: 37 g • Total Fat: 0 g • Protein: 5 g • Sodium: 360 mg • Fiber: 1 g •

Directions:

1. Begin by measuring 1 cup of starter and the remaining bread ingredients.
2. Add them to the bread machine pan.
3. Select the "Basic" or "White Bread" cycle on your bread machine with a medium or light crust color setting.

Classic Breads

Country-Style White Bread

	1-Pound Loaf	1½ - Pound Loaf	2-Pound Loaf	Nutrition:
Water	1½ cups	2¼ cups	3 cups	• Calories: 155
Extra-virgin olive oil	1⅓ tablespoons	2¼ tablespoons	3¼ tablespoons	• Total fat: 4 g
Plain bread flour	1 cup	1 ½ cups	2 cups	• Saturated fat: 1 g
White all-purpose flour	2½ cups	3¾ cups	5 cups	• Cholesterol: 0 mg • Carbohydrates: 18 g
Baking soda	⅓ teaspoon	½ teaspoon	½ teaspoon	• Dietary fiber: 3 g
Sugar	1⅓ teaspoon	2⅓ teaspoon	3 teaspoons	• Sodium: 390 mg
Salt	1 pinch	½ teaspoon	½ teaspoon	
Bread machine yeast	2⅓ teaspoon	3 teaspoons	5 teaspoons	• Protein: 3 g

Directions:

1. In order to ensure appropriate loading, either follow the indicated order of ingredients or refer to the handbook that came with your bread machine.
2.
   Set the crust shade to medium and program the rapid/express bake cycle.
   After the loaf has finished baking, move it to a wire rack and allow it to cool completely before slicing and serving.

Recommendations:

3. I used my bread maker's rapid/express baking mode for this recipe. However, by lowering the yeast to just 2¼ tablespoons, you can bake using the standard cycle.
4. Keep an eye on the dough as it kneads. Add a few teaspoons at a time of additional flour if it seems unduly sticky. Take a teaspoon or two at a time to add extra water if the dough seems too firm.

Honey and Milk White Bread

	1 Pound Loaf	1½ - Pound Loaf	2- Pound Loaf	Nutrition
Lukewarm whole milk	½ cup	1 cup	5 cups	• Calories: 162
Unsalted butter	¾ tablespoon	2 tablespoons	5 tablespoons	• Total fat: 1.7 g
Honey	¾ tablespoon	1½ tablespoons	5 tablespoons	• Saturated fat: 0.7 g
White all-purpose Flour	1½ cups	2¼ cups	3 cups	• Cholesterol: 2.2 mg
Salt	1 pinch	2 pinches	3 pinches	• Carbohydrates: 11 g
Bread machine yeast	¾ teaspoon	1½ teaspoons	5 teaspoons	• Dietary fiber: 0.7 g • Sodium: 42 mg • Protein: 2.9 g

Directions:

1. Follow the Directions: in your bread machine's instruction manual or add the ingredients to the machine in the sequence stated above.
2. Choose the settings for light crust and white bread.
3. Once the bread is baked, place it on a drying rack, let it cool, and then serve.

Butter Bread

	1-Pound Loaf	1½-Pound Loaf	2-Pound Loaf	Nutrition
Egg	1	1½	2	• Calories: 262
Lukewarm whole milk	1 cup	1¾ cups	2½ cups	• Total fat: 13.5 g
Unsalted butter, diced	½ cup	¾ cup	1 cup	• Saturated fat: 2.3 g • Cholesterol: 5.6 mg
Plain bread flour	2 cups	3¼ cups	41/3 cups	• Carbohydrates 29 g
Salt	1 pinch	1⅓ pinches	2 pinches	• Dietary fiber: 1.3 g
Sugar	1 pinch	1⅓ pinches	2 pinches	• Sodium: 40.3 mg
Instant dry yeast	2¼ teaspoons	3 teaspoons	4 teaspoons	• Protein: 6 g

Directions:

1. Follow the Directions: in your bread machine's instruction manual or add the ingredients to the machine in the sequence stated above.
2. Choose the medium crust function and the French setting.
3. Once the bread is baked, place it on a drying rack, let it cool, and then serve.

Advice
Use the white bread function on your bread machine if it doesn't have a French setting.

Basic White Bread

	1-Pound Loaf	1½-Pound Loaf	2-Pound Loaf	Nutrition
Lukewarm water	½ cup	¾ cup	1 cup	• Calories: 155
Lukewarm whole milk	¼ cup	½ cup	1/3 cup	• Total fat: 3 g
Unsalted butter, diced	1⅓ tablespoons	2¼ tablespoons	3¼ tablespoons	• Saturated fat: 1.3 g
White all-purpose Flour	1¾ cups	2¼ cups	3¾ cups	• Cholesterol: 5.5 mg • Carbohydrates: 1.3 g
Sugar	1½ tablespoon	2¼ tablespoons	3¼ tablespoons	• Dietary Fiber: 0.9 g
Salt	¾ teaspoon	1 teaspoon	1⅓ teaspoon	• Sodium: 130 mg
Instant dry yeast	¾ teaspoon	1 teaspoon	1⅓ teaspoon	• Protein: 2.1 ½

Directions:

1. Fill the bread maker with the ingredients in the above-listed order, or follow the Directions: in the manual that came with your bread maker.

2. Choose the medium crust function and the basic loaf option.

3. Once the bread is baked, place it on a drying rack, let it cool, and then serve.

Classic French bread

	1-Pound loaf	1½-Pound loaf	2-Pound loaf	Nutrition
Lukewarm water	1 cup	3 cups	5 cups	• Calories: 155
Sugar	1 teaspoon	1⅓ tablespoons	2¼ tablespoons	• Total Fat: 0.6 g
Salt	1 teaspoon	1⅓ teaspoon	1⅓ teaspoon	• Saturated fat: 0.1 • Cholesterol: 0 mg • Carbohydrates: 40.4 g
Plain bread flour	3¼ cups	32/3 cups	4 cups	• Dietary fiber: 1.1 g
Bread machine yeast	1 teaspoon	1⅓ teaspoon	1⅓ teaspoon	• Sodium: 290 mg • Protein: 6

Directions:

1. Fill the bread maker with the ingredients in the above-listed order, or follow the Directions: in the manual that came with your bread maker.

2. Choose the medium crust function and the basic loaf option.

3. When the bread is baked, place it on a drying rack, let it cool, and then serve.

Advice: If stored in a cloth bag and kept out of direct sunlight, this bread will stay fresh for up to four days.

Sourdough

	1-Pound Loaf	1½-Pound Loaf	2-Pound Loaf	Nutrition
Sourdough starter	½ cup	¾ cup	1 cup	• Calories: 180
Lukewarm water	1/3 cup	½ cup	¾ cup	• Total fat: 4.5 g
1Sugar	½ tablespoon	one tablespoon	one tablespoon	• Carbohydrates: 30 g
Active dry yeast	½ tablespoon	one tablespoon	one tablespoon	• Dietary fiber: 1.3 g
Plain bread flour	1½ cups	2¼ cups	3 cups	• Sodium: 460 mg
Vegetable oil	1⅓ tablespoons	2¼ tablespoons	3¼ tablespoons	• Protein: 4.5 g
Salt	1 teaspoon	1⅓ teaspoon	2 - teaspoons	

Ingredients for a sourdough starter	• 2 cups white, all-purpose flour • 1 teaspoon active dry yeast • 2 cups lukewarm water

How to make a sourdough starter

1. Transfer the ingredients onto a glass or ceramic dish. Make sure there is enough space in the dish for expansion.
2. Use an elastic band to secure the fabric that covers the dish in place.
3. Allow the starter to rest in a warm place for five days, stirring it once daily.
4. Your sourdough starter is now ready to use. Keep the remaining portion refrigerated and use as needed. You may keep the sourdough starter "alive" and use it to bake a few loaves by feeding it equal parts flour and water, letting it rest in a warm place, and using it as needed.

Bread Directions:

1. In the bread machine, combine the sourdough starter, water, sugar, and yeast. Mix thoroughly with a spatula.
2. Let the mixture rest for 10 minutes.
3. Add salt, oil, and bread flour.
4. Choose the medium crust function and the basic setting.
5. Once the bread is baked, place it on a drying rack, let it cool, and then serve.

Spice and Herb Bread

Awesome Rosemary Bread

	Ingredients	Nutrition
1 ½-Pound Loaf	• ¾ cup + one tablespoon water • 1 2/3¼ tablespoons melted butter, cooled • 2¼ teaspoons sugar • 1 teaspoon salt • one tablespoon fresh rosemary, chopped • 2 cups white bread flour • 1 1/3 teaspoons instant yeast	• Calories: 127 • Carbohydrates: 25 g • Fiber: 1 g • Protein: 4 g • Fat: 3 g • Sodium: 230 mg

Directions:

1. Add all the ingredients to your bread machine, ensuring you follow the manufacturer's Directions: .

2. Program your bread machine to Basic/White Bread and set the crust type to Medium.

3. Press the START button.

4. Wait until the cycle is finished.

5. After the loaf is done, remove the pan and let the loaf cool for 5 minutes.

Original Italian Herb Bread

	Ingredients	Nutrition
1 ½-Pound Loaf	• 1 cup water • ½ cup olive brine • 1⅓ tablespoons butter • 3¼ tablespoons sugar • 2¼ teaspoons salt • 5 1/3 cups flour • 2¼ teaspoons bread machine yeast • 1 olive, black/green • 1⅓ teaspoon Italian herbs	•Calories. 180 •Carbohydrates: 18 g •Fiber: 1 g •Fat: 7 g •Protein: 1 g •Sodium: 320 mg

Directions:

1. Slice the olives into pieces.
2. Place all ingredients into your bread machine, following the manufacturer's Directions: carefully.
3. Choose a Medium crust and set your bread maker to bake French bread.
4. When the machine beeps, add the olives.
5. Wait until the cycle completes.
6. After the loaf is ready, remove the pan and allow the loaf to cool for 5-7 minutes.

Lovely Aromatic Lavender Bread

	Ingredients	Nutrition
1-Pound Loaf	• ¾ cup milk • one tablespoon melted butter, cooled • one tablespoon sugar • ¾ teaspoon salt • 1 teaspoon fresh lavender flower, chopped • ⅓ teaspoon lemon zest • ⅓ teaspoon fresh thyme, chopped • 2 cups white bread flour • ¾ teaspoon instant yeast	•Calories: 155 •Carbohydrates: 27 g •Fiber: 1 g •Protein: 4 g •Fat: 3 g •Sodium: 180 mg

Directions:

1. Combine all ingredients in your bread machine, ensuring you follow the manufacturer's Directions: carefully.
2. Choose a Medium crust and set your bread maker to bake Basic/White Bread.
3. Wait for the cycle to complete.
4. After the loaf is ready, remove the pan and allow the loaf to cool for 5 minutes.

Cinnamon & Dried Fruits Bread

	Ingredients	Nutrition
1-Pound Loaf	• 2¾ cups flour • ¾ cup water • 1½ cups dried fruits • 4 tablespoons sugar • 2½ tablespoons butter • one tablespoon milk powder • 1 teaspoon cinnamon • ½ teaspoon ground nutmeg • ⅓ teaspoon vanillin • ½ cup peanuts • powdered sugar, for sprinkling • 1 teaspoon salt • 1½ teaspoon bread machine yeast	• Calories: 315 • Carbohydrates: 65 g • Fiber: 1 g • Protein: 5 g • Fat: 4 g • Sodium: 230 mg

Directions:
1. Combine all ingredients in your bread machine, following the manufacturer's Directions: carefully (except peanuts and powdered sugar).
2. Select a Medium crust and set your bread maker to bake Basic/White Bread.
3. When the bread maker beeps, moisten the dough with a bit of water and add peanuts.
4. Wait for the cycle to complete.
5. Once the loaf is ready, remove the pan and let the loaf cool for 5 minutes.

Herbal Garlic Cream Cheese Delight

	Ingredients	Nutrition
1-Pound Loaf	• 1/3 cup water • 1/3 cup herb and garlic cream cheese mix, at room temp • 1 whole egg, beaten, at room temp • 4 teaspoons melted butter, cooled • one tablespoon sugar • 2/3 teaspoon salt • 2 cups white bread flour • 1 teaspoon instant yeast	• Calories:182 • Carbohydrates: 27 g • Fiber: 3 g • Protein: 5 g • Fat: 6 g • Sodium: 200 mg

Directions:
1. Combine all ingredients in your bread machine according to the manufacturer's Directions: .
2. Choose a Medium crust and set the machine to make Basic or White Bread.
3. Allow the cycle to complete.
4. After baking, remove the pan and let the loaf cool for 5-7 minutes.

Oregano Mozza-Cheese Bread

1 ½ -Pound loaf

	Ingredients	Nutrition
1 ½ -Pound loaf	• 1 cup (milk + egg) mixture • ½ cup mozzarella cheese • 2¼ cups flour • ¾ cup whole grain flour • 2¼ tablespoons sugar • 1 teaspoon salt • 2¼ teaspoons oregano • 1⅓ teaspoon dry yeast	• Calories: 190 • Carbohydrates: 40 g • Fiber: 1 g • Protein: 7.7 g • Fat: 2.1 g • Sodium: 220 mg

Directions:

1. Combine all ingredients in your bread machine, following the manufacturer's Directions: carefully.

2. Choose the Dark crust option and set the program to Basic/White Bread.

3. Allow the cycle to complete.

4. After baking, remove the pan and let the loaf cool for 5-7 minutes.

5. Gently shake the pan to release the loaf.

Cumin Tossed Fancy Bread

	Ingredients	Nutrition
2 -Pound loaf	• 5 1/3 cups wheat flour • 1⅓ teaspoon salt • 1⅓ tablespoons sugar • one tablespoon dry yeast • 1¾ cups water • 2¼ tablespoons cumin • 3¼ tablespoons sunflower oil	• Calories: 161 • Carbohydrates: 67 g • Fiber: 2g • Protein: 9.5 g • Fat: 7 g • Sodium: 220 mg

Directions:

1. Begin by adding warm water to the bread machine pan.
2. Next, add salt, sugar, and sunflower oil.
3. After adding yeast, sift in wheat flour.
4. Choose a Medium crust and set your bread maker to bake French bread.
5. When the bread maker beeps, add cumin.
6. Allow the cycle to complete.
7. After baking, remove the pan and let the loaf cool for 5-7 minutes.

Potato Rosemary Loaf

	Ingredients	Nutrition
1 ½ -Pound loaf	• 4 cups wheat flour • one tablespoon sugar • one tablespoon sunflower oil • 1⅓ teaspoon salt • 1½ cups water • 1 teaspoon dry yeast • 1 cup mashed potatoes, ground through a sieve • crushed rosemary to taste	• Calories: 276 • Carbohydrates: 54 g • Fiber: 1 g • Protein: 13 g • Fat: 3 g • Sodium: 220 mg

Directions:

1. Place flour, salt, and sugar into the bread maker pan and attach the mixing paddle.
2. Add water and sunflower oil.
3. Add yeast as instructed.
4. Choose a Medium crust and set your bread maker to Bread with Filling mode.
5. When the bread maker beeps and signals to add more ingredients, open the lid and add mashed potatoes and chopped rosemary.
6. Allow the cycle to complete.
7. After baking, remove the pan and let the loaf cool for 5 minutes.

Delicious Honey Lavender Bread

	Ingredients	Nutrition
1 ½ -Pound loaf	• 1½ cups wheat flour • 2 1/3 cups whole meal flour • 1 teaspoon fresh yeast • 1½ cups water • 1 teaspoon lavender • 1⅓ tablespoons honey • 1 teaspoon salt	• Calories: 226 • Carbohydrates: 46 g • Fiber: 1 g • Protein: 7.5 g • Fat: 1.5 g • Sodium: 230 mg

Directions:
1. Begin by sifting both types of flour into a bowl and mixing them together.
2. Add all of the ingredients to your bread machine, ensuring to follow the manufacturer's instructions carefully.
3. Choose a Medium crust and set your bread maker to bake Basic/White Bread.
4. Wait until the cycle completes.
5. Once the loaf is ready, remove the pan from the machine and let the loaf cool for 5-7 minutes.

Inspiring Cinnamon Bread

	Ingredients	Nutrition
1-Pound loaf	• 2/3 cup milk • 1 whole egg, beaten • 3¼ tablespoons melted butter, cooled • 1/3 cup sugar • 1/3 teaspoon salt • 1 teaspoon ground cinnamon • 2 cups white bread flour • 1 1/3 teaspoons active dry yeast	• Calories: 191 • Carbohydrates: 34 g • Fiber: 1 g • Protein: 5 g • Fat: 5 g • Sodium: 60 mg

Directions:
1. Add all of the ingredients to your bread machine, ensuring to follow the Directions: of the manufacturer carefully.
2. Choose a Medium crust and set your bread maker to bake Basic/White Bread.
3. Wait until the cycle completes.
4. Once the loaf is ready, remove the pan from the machine and let the loaf cool for 5-7 minutes.
5. Remove the loaf from the pan.

Lavender Buttermilk Bread

	Ingredients	Nutrition
1 ½ -Pound loaf	• ½ cup water • ½ cup buttermilk • ¼ cup olive oil • 3¼ tablespoons finely chopped fresh lavender leaves • 1 ⅓ teaspoons finely chopped fresh lavender flowers • grated zest of 1 lemon • 4 cups bread flour • 2¼ teaspoons salt • 2 ¾ teaspoons bread machine yeast	• Calories: 175 • Carbohydrates: 27 g • Fat: 5 g • Protein: 3 g • Calories: 180 • Sodium: 480 mg

Directions:
1. Add each ingredient to the bread machine in the order and temperature recommended by the manufacturer.
2. Close the cover, select the medium crust option for basic bread, then press the start button on your bread maker.
3. Once the bread machine has finished baking, remove the loaf and transfer it to a cooling rack.

Cajun Bread

	Ingredients	Nutrition
1-Pound loaf	• ½ cup water • ¼ cup chopped onion • ¼ cup chopped green bell pepper • 2¼ teaspoons finely chopped garlic • 2¼ teaspoons soft butter • 2 cups bread flour • one tablespoon sugar • 1 teaspoon Cajun • ½ teaspoon salt • 1 teaspoon active dry yeast	• Calories: 180 • Carbohydrates: 23 g • Fat: 4 g • Protein: 5 g • Sodium: 120 mg

Directions:
1. Add each ingredient to the bread machine in the specified order and temperature recommended by the manufacturer.
2. Close the lid, select Medium Crust for the basic bread option, and start the machine.
3. Once the bread machine has finished baking, remove the loaf and transfer it to a cooling rack.

Turmeric Bread

	Ingredients	Nutrition
1 ½ -Pound loaf	• 1 teaspoon dried yeast • 4 cups strong white flour • 1 teaspoon turmeric powder • 2¼ teaspoons beetroot powder • 2¼ tablespoons olive oil • 1⅓ teaspoon salt • 1 teaspoon chili flakes • 1½ cups water	• Calories: 172 • Carbohydrates: 24 g • Fat: 3 g • Protein: 3 g • Sodium: 360 mg

Directions:
1. Add each ingredient to the bread machine in the specified order and temperature recommended by the manufacturer.
2. Start the machine, close the lid, and select the medium crust option for basic bread.
3. Once the bread machine has finished baking, remove the loaf and transfer it to a cooling rack.

Rosemary Cranberry Pecan Bread

	Ingredients	Nutrition
2-Pound loaf	• 1 1/3 cups water, plus • 2¼ tablespoons water • 2¼ tablespoons butter • 2¼ teaspoons salt • 4 cups bread flour • ¾ cup dried sweetened cranberries • ¾ cup toasted chopped pecans • 2¼ tablespoons non-fat powdered milk • ¼ cup sugar • 2¼ teaspoons yeast	• Calories: 171 • Carbohydrates: 13 g • Fat: 5 g • Protein: 9 g • Sodium: 480 mg

Directions:
1. Add each ingredient to the bread machine in the specified order and temperature recommended by the manufacturer.
2. Close the lid, select the default bread option (medium crust), and press the start button.
3. Once the bread machine has finished baking, remove the loaf and transfer it to a cooling rack.

Sesame French Bread

	Ingredients	Nutrition
1 ½ -Pound loaf	• 1½ cups water • one tablespoon butter, softened • 3 cups bread flour • 2¼ teaspoons sugar • 1 teaspoon salt • 2¼ teaspoons yeast • 2¼ tablespoons sesame seeds toasted	• Calories: 165 • Carbohydrates: 18 g • Fat: 3 g • Protein: 6 g • Sodium: 180 mg

Directions:
1. Add each ingredient to the bread machine in the specified order and temperature recommended by the manufacturer.
2. Select the French bread setting, choose medium crust, and press start.
3. Once the bread machine has finished baking, remove the loaf and transfer it to a cooling rack.

Savoury Herb Blend Bread

	Ingredients	Nutrition
1½-Pound Loaf	• 1 cup almond flour • 1 cup water • ½ cup coconut flour • 1 cup parmesan cheese • ¾ teaspoon baking powder • 3 eggs • 3¼ tablespoons coconut oil • ½ tablespoon rosemary • ½ teaspoon thyme, ground • ½ teaspoon sage, ground • ½ teaspoon oregano • ½ teaspoon garlic powder • ½ teaspoon onion powder • ⅓ teaspoon salt	• Calories: 180 • Carbohydrates: 6 g • Protein: 9 g • Fat: 15 g • Sodium: 155 mg

Directions:

1. Beat eggs and coconut oil until light before adding them to the bread machine pan.
2. Add all remaining ingredients to the bread machine pan.
3. Activate the gluten-free setting on the bread maker.
4. Once the bread is finished, remove the bread machine pan.
5. Allow the bread to cool slightly before transferring it to a cooling rack.

Semolina Bread

	Ingredients	Nutrition
1-Pound loaf	• 1 cup almond fine flour • 1 cup semolina flour • 1 teaspoon yeast • 1 egg • 1 teaspoon salt • 2¼ teaspoons Stevia powder • 2¼ teaspoons Olive oil extra • 1 cup warm water • 2¼ teaspoons sesame seeds	• Calories: 180 • Carbohydrates: 2.3 g • Protein: 5 g • Fat: 1 g • Sodium: 200 mg

Directions:

1. In a mixing bowl, combine almond flour, semolina flour, salt, and stevia powder.
2. In another bowl, mix the egg, extra virgin olive oil, and warm water.
3. Following your machine's manual, pour the ingredients into the bread pan and add the yeast as instructed.
4. Insert the bread pan into the machine. Choose the basic bread setting, select the bread size, and if applicable, set the crust type. Close the machine's lid and press start.
5. When the bread cycle is complete, remove the lid and sprinkle sesame seeds on top. Allow it to cool briefly.
6. Use oven mitts to remove the bread pan from the machine. Carefully transfer the bread from the pan using a stainless spatula, then place the pan upside down on a metal rack to cool before slicing.

Seeded Bread

	Ingredients	Nutrition
1-Pound loaf	• 2¼ tablespoons chia seeds • ½ cup water • ⅓ teaspoon salt • 7 large eggs • ½ teaspoon Xanthan gum • 2 cups almond flour • 1 teaspoon baking powder • ½ cup unsalted butter • 3¼ tablespoons sesame seeds • 2¼ tablespoons olive oil	• Calories: 190 • Fat: 4 g • Carbohydrates: 4 g • Protein: 6 g • Sodium: 150 mg

Directions:

1. Add all the ingredients to the bread machine, close the lid, and select the Bread mode.
2. Once the baking cycle is complete, remove the bread from the machine and slice it into at least 5 slices.
3. This seeded bread can be stored in the fridge for up to 5 days.

Macadamia Bread

	Ingredients	Nutrition
1-Pound loaf	• ¼ cup almond flour • ½ cup water • 1 cup macadamia nuts • 2¼ tablespoons flax meal • 1 teaspoon baking powder • 2 scoops of whey Protein: powder • 4 eggs • 2 egg whites • one tablespoon lemon juice • ¼ cup butter, melted	• Calories: 257 • Fat: 22.2 g • Carbohydrates: 4.5 g • Protein: 11.5 g • Sodium: 20 mg

Directions:

1. Fill the bread maker with all the ingredients.
2. Select the Express Bake option and close the lid.
3. Once the bread has finished baking, remove it from the machine and slice it into at least five slices.

Garlic, Herb, and Cheese Bread

	Ingredients	Nutrition
1 ½-Pound Loaf	• ½ cup ghee • 6 eggs • 2 cups almond flour • one tablespoon baking powder • ½ teaspoon Xanthan gum • 1 cup cheddar cheese, shredded • one tablespoon garlic powder • one tablespoon parsley • ½ tablespoon oregano • ½ teaspoon salt	• Calories: 186 • Carbohydrates: 4 g • Protein: 5 g • Fat: 13 g • Sodium: 120 mg

Directions:

1. Gently whisk together the eggs and melted ghee, then pour them into the bread machine pan.
2. Add the remaining ingredients to the pan.
3. Set your bread machine to the gluten-free program.
4. Once the bread is finished baking, remove the bread pan from the machine.
5. Allow the bread to cool slightly before transferring it to a cooling rack.
6. Store the bread in the refrigerator for up to 5 days.

Parsley Cheddar Bread

	Ingredients	Nutrition
2-Pound Loaf	• one tablespoon butter • 2¼ tablespoons coconut flour • 1 large egg • one tablespoon heavy whipping cream • 2¼ tablespoons water • ¼ cup cheddar cheese • 1 teaspoon garlic powder • 1 teaspoon onion powder • 1 teaspoon dried parsley • 1teaspoon pink Himalayan salt • 1teaspoon black pepper • ⅓ teaspoon baking powder	• Calories: 183 • Total Fat 4 g • Cholesterol: 27 mg • Sodium: 39 mg • Carbohydrates: 9.3 g • Sugar 3.1 g • Fiber: 4.6 g • Protein: 1 g

Directions:

1. Heat the butter until melted.
2. Slowly stir in the seasonings, baking powder, and coconut flour until the mixture is smooth.
3. Combine the cream, cheese, water, and egg, then whisk together.
4. Beat the mixture until smooth, then microwave for 3 minutes.
5. Allow the bread to cool before serving.

Orangey Almond Bacon Bread

	Ingredients	Nutrition
1-Pound Loaf	• 1½ cups almond flour • ½ cup water • one tablespoon baking powder • 7 oz bacon, diced • 2 eggs • 1½ cups cheddar cheese, shredded • 4 tablespoons butter, melted • 1/3 cup sour cream	• Calories: 307 • Fat: 26 g • Carbohydrate: 3 g • Protein: 1 g • Sodium: 120 mg

Directions:

1. Place all ingredients into the bread machine.
2. Close the lid and set it to the Sweet Bread mode.
3. After the baking cycle completes, remove the bread and let it cool for about 5 minutes.

Rosemary Garlic Dinner Rolls

	Ingredients	Nutrition
1-Pound Loaf	• ½ teaspoon baking powder • ½ cup water • 1/3 cup ground flax seed • 1 cup mozzarella cheese, shredded • 1 cup almond flour • 1 teaspoon rosemary, minced • A pinch of salt • 1 oz. cream cheese • 1 egg, beaten • one tablespoon butter • 1 teaspoon garlic, minced	• Calories: 180 • Fat: 18 g • Carbohydrate: 5,5 g • Protein: 1,3 g • Sodium: 120 mg

Directions:

1. Place all ingredients in the bread machine.
2. Select the Dough setting. Once the dough cycle is complete, transfer the dough to a floured surface and shape it into a ball.
3. Shape the dough into a log and cut it into six pieces. Arrange them on a greased baking sheet.
4. In a bowl, combine rosemary, garlic, and butter. Brush half of this mixture over the biscuits.
5. Preheat the oven to 350°F and bake for 12-15 minutes.
6. Brush the biscuits with the remaining mixture and sprinkle with salt before serving.

Lavender Bread

	Ingredients	Nutrition
1-Pound Loaf	• ¾ cup lukewarm milk • one tablespoon butter, melted • one tablespoon brown sugar • ¾ teaspoon salt • 1 teaspoon fresh lavender flower, chopped • ⅓ teaspoon lemon zest • ⅓ teaspoon fresh thyme, chopped • 2 cups all-purpose flour, sifted • ¾ teaspoon active dry yeast	• Calories: 163 • Total Fat: 3 g • Saturated Fat: 1 g • Cholesterol: 4 g • Sodium: 218 mg • Carbohydrates: 25.3 g • Dietary Fiber: 0.9 g • Total Sugars: 1.3 g • Protein: 3.4 g • Vitamin D: 1 mcg • Calcium 1 mg • Potassium: 40 mg

Directions:
1. Gather all the ingredients for your bread and the necessary measuring tools.
2. Measure each ingredient carefully into the bread machine pan.
3. Add all ingredients to the bread machine pan following the manual's Directions: .
4. Close the cover securely.
5. Select the BASIC program on your bread machine and choose MEDIUM crust color.
6. Press the START button.
7. Wait for the program to complete.
8. Once finished, remove the bread pan from the machine and allow the loaf to cool for 5 minutes.
9. Remove the loaf from the pan and let it cool for an additional 30 minutes on a cooling rack.

Onion Bacon Bread

	Ingredients	Nutrition
2-Pound Loaf	• 1½ cups lukewarm water • 2¼ tablespoons sugar • 3 teaspoons active dry yeast • 4½ cups wheat flour • 1 whole egg • 2¼ teaspoons kosher salt • one tablespoon olive oil • 3 small onions, chopped and lightly toasted • 1 cup bacon, chopped	• Calories: 391 • Fat: 9.7 g • Cholesterol: 31 g • Sodium: 480 mg • Carbohydrates: 59.9 g • Fiber: 2.1 g

Directions:

1. Gather all ingredients and necessary measuring tools.
2. Carefully measure all ingredients into the bread machine pan, excluding bacon and onion.
3. Follow the bread machine manual's order to place ingredients into the bucket.
4. Close the cover securely.
5. Set the bread machine to BASIC program and Medium crust color.
6. Press the START button.
7. Add bacon and onion when prompted by the machine.
8. Wait for the program to complete.
9. Once finished, remove the bread pan and allow the loaf to cool for 5 minutes.

Sunflower & Flax Seed Bread

	Ingredients	Nutrition
2-Pound Loaf	• 1 1/3 cups water • 2¼ tablespoons butter • 3¼ tablespoons honey • 1½ cups bread flour • 1 1/3 cups whole wheat flour • 1 teaspoon salt • 1 teaspoon active dry yeast • ½ cup flax seed • ½ cup sunflower seeds	• Calories: 180 • Carbohydrates: 36.6 g • Fat: 5.7 g • Protein: 6. 6 g • Sodium: 230 mg

Directions:

1. Place all ingredients, excluding sunflower seeds, into the bread machine pan.
2. Choose the basic setting, then select light/medium crust, and start the machine.
3. Just before the final kneading cycle starts, add the sunflower seeds.
4. Once the bread is done, remove the pan from the machine and let it cool for 4-6 minutes before slicing and serving.

Healthy Spelt Bread

	Ingredients	Nutrition
1½-Pound Loaf	• ¼ cups milk • 2¼ tablespoons sugar • 2¼ tablespoons olive oil • 1 teaspoon salt • 4 cups spelt flour • 2⅓ teaspoon yeast	• Calories: 223 • Carbohydrates: 40.3 g • Fat: 4.5 g • Protein: 9.3 g • Sodium: 230 mg •

Directions:

1. Place all ingredients into the bread machine following the manufacturer's Directions: .
2. Select the machine's default bread setting, typically light to medium crust, and start it.
3. Once the bread is finished baking, remove the pan from the machine.
4. Allow it to cool for 4-6 minutes, then slice and serve.

Nutritious 9-Grain Bread

	Ingredients	Nutrition
1-Pound Loaf	• ¾ cup+2¼ tablespoons warm water • 1 cup whole wheat flour • 1 cup bread flour • 9½ cups, crushed 9-grain cereal • 1 teaspoon salt • one tablespoon butter • 2¼ tablespoons sugar • one tablespoon milk powder • 2¼ teaspoons active dry yeast	• Calories: 162 • Carbohydrates: 25 g • Fat: 1.7 g • Protein: 4.1 g • Sodium: 155 mg

Directions:

1. Place all ingredients into the bread machine.
2. Select the whole wheat setting and choose a light/medium crust. Start the machine.
3. Once the bread is finished baking, remove the bread pan from the machine.
4. Allow the loaf to cool for 5 minutes, then slice and serve.

Oatmeal Sunflower Bread

	Ingredients	Nutrition
1½-Pound Loaf	• 1 cup water • ¼ cup honey • 2¼ tablespoons softened butter • 3 cups bread flour • ½ cup old fashioned oats • 2¼ tablespoons milk powder • 1 ⅓ teaspoons salt • 2 ⅓ teaspoons active dry yeast • ½ cup sunflower seeds	• Calories: 185 • Carbohydrates: 39 g • Fat: 4.3 g • Protein: 5.4 g • Sodium: 300 mg

Directions:

1. Place all ingredients except for sunflower seeds into the bread machine pan.
2. Select the basic setting, then choose a light/medium crust, and press start. Just before the final kneading cycle begins, add the sunflower seeds.
3. Once the bread is finished baking, remove the bread pan from the machine.
4. Allow the loaf to cool for 4-6 minutes, then slice and serve.

Cornmeal Whole Wheat Bread

	Ingredients	Nutrition
2-Pound Loaf	• 2⅓ teaspoon active dry yeast • 1 1/3 cups water • 2¼ tablespoons sugar • 1 egg, lightly beaten • 2¼ tablespoons butter • 1 ⅓ teaspoon salt • ¾cup cornmeal • ¾cup whole wheat flour • 2¾cups bread flour	• Calories: 218 • Carbohydrates: 41 g • Fat: 3.3 g • Protein: 7.1 g • Sodium: 230 mg

Directions:

1. Place all ingredients into the bread machine pan following the bread machine manufacturer's instructions.
2. Choose the basic bread setting with a medium crust and start the machine. Remove the bread pan from the machine once the bread is finished.
3. Allow it to cool for 4-6 minutes , then slice and serve.

Delicious Cranberry Bread

	Ingredients	Nutrition
2-Pound Loaf	• 1½ cups warm water • 2¼ tablespoons brown sugar • 1⅓ teaspoon salt • 2¼ tablespoons olive oil • 4 cups flour • 1⅓ teaspoon cinnamon • 1⅓ teaspoon cardamom • 1 cup dried cranberries • 2¼ teaspoons yeast	• Calories: 223 • Carbohydrates: 41.7 g • Fat: 3.3 g • Protein: 5.5 g • Sodium: 320 mg

Directions:

1. Place all ingredients into the bread machine in the specified order.
2. Select the sweet bread setting with a light/medium crust and start the machine. Once the bread is finished, remove the bread pan from the machine.
3. Allow the loaf to cool for 2-3 minute before slicing and serving.

Coffee Raisin Bread

	Ingredients	Nutrition
2-Pound Loaf	• 2⅓ teaspoon active dry yeast • ⅓ teaspoon ground cloves • ⅓ teaspoon ground allspice • 1 teaspoon ground cinnamon • 3¼ tablespoons sugar • 1 egg, lightly beaten • 3¼ tablespoons olive oil • 1 cup strong brewed coffee • 3 cups bread flour • ¾ cup raisins • 1⅓ teaspoon salt	• Calories: 230 • Carbohydrates: 41.5 g • Fat: 5.1 g • Protein: 5.3 g • Sodium: 40 mg

Directions:

1. Place all ingredients, excluding raisins, into the bread machine pan.
2. Select the basic setting, then choose a light/medium crust, and press start. Add raisins just before the final kneading cycle begins.
3. Once the bread is done, remove the bread pan from the machine. Allow the loaf to cool for 4-6 minute, then slice and serve.

Healthy Multigrain Bread

	Ingredients	Nutrition
1 ½-Pound Loaf	• 1¼ cups water • 2¼ tablespoons butter • 1 1/3 cups bread flour • 1½ cups whole wheat flour • 1 cup multigrain cereal • 3¼ tablespoons brown sugar • 1⅓ teaspoons salt • 2⅓ teaspoon yeast	• Calories: 169 • Carbohydrates: 29.3 g • Fat: 2.9 g • Protein: 4.6 g • Sodium: 260 mg

Directions:

1. Place all listed ingredients into the bread machine pan. Choose the basic bread setting with a light/medium crust and start the machine.
2. Once the bread is finished, remove the bread pan from the machine. Allow the loaf to cool for 4-6 minutes, then slice and serve.

Italian Pine Nut Bread

	Ingredients	Nutrition
2-Pound Loaf	<ul><li>1 cup+ 2¼ tablespoons water</li><li>3 cups bread flour</li><li>2¼ tablespoons sugar</li><li>1 teaspoon salt</li><li>5 teaspoons active dry yeast</li><li>1/3 cup basil pesto</li><li>2¼ tablespoons flour</li><li>1/3 cup pine nuts</li></ul>	<ul><li>Calories: 180</li><li>Carbohydrates: 34 g</li><li>Fat: 3.5g</li><li>Protein: 4.1 g</li><li>Sodium: 230 mg</li></ul>

Directions:

1. Mix basil pesto and flour in a small container until well blended. Stir in pine nuts. In the bread machine pan, combine water, bread flour, sugar, salt, and yeast.
2. Select the basic setting with a medium crust and press start. Add the basil pesto mixture just before the final kneading cycle.
3. Once the loaf is done, remove the bread pan from the machine. Let it cool for 4-6 minute, then slice and serve.

Whole Wheat Raisin Bread

	Ingredients	Nutrition
1½-Pound Loaf	• 3½ cups whole wheat flour • 2¼ teaspoons dry yeast • 2 eggs, lightly beaten • ¼ cup butter, softened • ¾ cup water • 1/3 cup milk • 1 teaspoon salt • 1/3 cup sugar • 4 teaspoons cinnamon • 1 cup raisins	• Calories: 290 • Carbohydrates: 53 g • Fat: 6.2g • Protein: 6.1 g • Sodium: 230 mg •

Directions:

1. Fill the bread pan with the water, milk, butter, and eggs. Add the remaining ingredients to the bread pan, excluding the yeast. Make a tiny well in the flour and add the yeast, being careful not to let it come into contact with any liquid.
2. Select a light or medium crust, turn on the machine, and choose the whole wheat setting. Remove the bread pan from the machine after the loaf is finished.
3. Let it cool for five minutes, then slice and serve.

Sun Vegetable Bread

	Ingredients	Nutrition
1½-Pound Loaf	• 2 cups (250 g) wheat flour • 2 cups (250 g) whole-wheat flour • 2¼ teaspoons panifarin • 2¼ teaspoons yeast • 1⅓ teaspoon salt • one tablespoon sugar • one tablespoon paprika dried pounds • 2¼ tablespoons dried beets • one tablespoon dried garlic • 1½ cups water • one tablespoon vegetable oil	• Calories: 253 • Total Fat: 2.6 g • Saturated Fat: 0.5 g • Cholesterol: 0 g • Sodium: 444 mg • Carbohydrate: 49.6 g • Dietary Fiber: 2.6 g • Sugars: 0.6 g • Protein: 7.3 g

Directions:

1. Adjust the baking program to 4 hours and select a medium crust color.
2. Monitor the kneading phase closely to ensure the dough becomes smooth and soft.

Peaches and Cream Bread

	Ingredients	Nutrition
-	• ½ cup canned peaches, drained and chopped • ¼ cup heavy whipping cream, at 80°F • 1 egg, at room temperature • one tablespoon melted butter cooled • 1⅓ tablespoons sugar • ¾ teaspoon salt • ⅓ teaspoon ground cinnamon • 1 ½ teaspoon ground nutmeg • ¼ cup whole-wheat flour • 1¾ cups white bread flour • ¾ teaspoons bread machine or instant yeast	• Calories: 253 • Carbohydrates: 27 g • Total Fat: 4 g • Protein: 5 g • Sodium: 180 mg • Fiber: 1 g

Directions:
1. Follow the instructions provided by your bread machine manufacturer to add all ingredients.
2. Choose the Basic White bread setting, opt for a medium crust, and start the machine.
3. Once the cycle completes, remove the bread bucket from the machine.
4. Allow it to cool for five minutes.
5. Gently shake the bucket to release the loaf, then transfer it to a cooling rack.

Tomato Onion Bread

	Ingredients	Nutrition
1-Pound Loaf	• 2 cups all-purpose flour • 1 cup whole meal flour • ½ cup warm water • 2¼ tablespoons milk • 3¼ tablespoons olive oil • 2¼ tablespoons sugar • 1 teaspoon salt • 2¼ teaspoons dry yeast • ½ teaspoon baking powder • 5 sun-dried tomatoes • 1 onion • ⅓ teaspoon black pepper	• Calories: 241 • Total Fat: 6.4 g • Saturated Fat: 1.1 g • Cholesterol: 1 g • Sodium: 305 mg • Carbohydrates: 40 g • Dietary Fiber: 3.5 g • Sugars: 6.1 g • Protein: 6 g

Directions:
1. Begin by preparing all the required ingredients. Sauté finely chopped onions until they are golden brown. Slice the sun-dried tomatoes into small pieces.
2. Fill the basin of the bread maker with the liquid ingredients. Make sure the flour covers the liquids by layering it on top. Add the sun-dried tomatoes and sautéed onions. Avoid letting the yeast and baking powder come into contact with the liquid when you sprinkle them over the flour.
3. Choose "Bread with Additives" as the preferred baking method, then start the cycle. The dough will be kneaded slowly by the bread maker.

Tomato Bread

	Ingredients	Nutrition
1½-Pound Loaf	• 3¼ tablespoons tomato paste • 1½ cups (340 ml) water • 4 1/3 cups (560 g) flour • 1⅓ tablespoons vegetable oil • 2¼ teaspoons sugar • 2¼ teaspoons salt • 1⅓ teaspoon dry yeast • ½ teaspoon oregano, dried • ½ teaspoon ground sweet paprika	• Calories: 218 • Total Fat: 3.3 g • Saturated Fat: 0.6 g • Cholesterol: 0 g • Sodium: 440 mg • Carbohydrate: 54.3 g • Dietary Fiber: 2.2 g • Sugars: 1.7 g • Protein: 7.6 g •

Directions:

1. Begin by diluting the tomato paste in warm water. Adjust the amount of tomato paste according to your preference, but ensure it is at least one tablespoon for color consistency.
2. Prepare the spices, including oregano, Provencal herbs, and paprika, to taste.
3. Sift the flour to aerate it, then mix in the spices thoroughly.
4. Add vegetable oil to the bread maker container, followed by the diluted tomato paste, sugar, salt, and spiced flour mixture. Finally, add the yeast.
5. Start the bread maker on the Basic program with a Medium crust setting.
6. Once the baking cycle is complete, turn off the bread maker and remove the bread container. Transfer the hot bread to a cooling rack and let it cool for an hour.

Squash Carrot Bread

	Ingredients	Nutrition
1-Pound Loaf	• 1 small zucchini • 1 baby carrot • 1 cup whey • 1 ½ cups (11g) white wheat flour • ¾ cup (10 g) whole wheat flour • ¾ cup (10 g) rye flour • 2¼ tablespoons vegetable oil • 1 teaspoon yeast, fresh • 1 teaspoon salt • ½ teaspoon sugar	• Calories: 180 • Total Fat: 4.3 g • Saturated Fat: 0.1 ½ g • Cholesterol: 0 g • Sodium: 313 mg • Carbohydrates: 39.1 g • Dietary Fiber: 4.1 g • Total Sugars: 2.7 g • Protein: 6.6 g

Directions:

1. Cut or dice the carrots and zucchini into pieces approximately 15 mm (1/2 inch) in size.
2. In a frying pan, warm the vegetable oil and sauté the vegetables over medium heat until soft. Season with salt and pepper if desired.
3. Transfer the cooked vegetables to a flat plate to cool quickly.
4. Mix the yeast with the serum.
5. Combine all types of flour, the yeast mixture, salt, and sugar in a mixing bowl.
6. Knead the dough using the Dough for Rolls program.
7. At the end of the kneading cycle, add the cooled vegetables to the dough.
8. After adding the vegetables, the dough will become moister. Let it ferment for about an hour until it doubles in volume.
9. Transfer the dough onto a thickly floured surface and shape it into a loaf. Place it in an oiled form.

10.   Cover the form with plastic wrap and let it rise for 1 to 1 1/3 hours.

Curd Onion Bread with Sesame Seeds

	Ingredients	Nutrition
1½-Pound Loaf	• ¾ cup water • 3 2/3 cups wheat flour • 3/4 cup cottage cheese • 2¼ tablespoons softened butter • 2¼ tablespoons sugar • 1⅓ teaspoon salt • 1⅓ tablespoons sesame seeds • 2¼ tablespoons dried onions • 1⅓ teaspoons dry yeast	• Calories: 277 • Total Fat: 4.7 g • Saturated Fat: 2.3 g • Cholesterol: 9 g • Sodium: 347mg • Dietary Fiber: 1.7 g • Sugars: 3.3 g • Protein: 9.4 g • Carbohydrates: 41 g

Directions:

1. Follow the bread maker's instructions for placing the ingredients.
2. Select the Basic program and start the bread maker.

Banana Bread

Ingredients	Nutrition
• 1 teaspoon baking powder • 1 cup water • ½ teaspoon baking soda • 2 bananas, peeled and halved lengthwise • 2 cups all-purpose flour • 2 eggs • 3¼ tablespoons vegetable oil • ¾ cup white sugar	• Calories: 350 • Carbohydrate: 40 g • Fat: 13 g • Protein

Directions:

1. Place the ingredients into the bread pan and select the dough setting. Start and mix for 3-5 minutes.
2. After mixing, smooth out the top of the dough.
3. Use a spatula to smooth the top, then select the bake setting. Start and bake for approximately 50 minutes. Test for doneness by inserting a toothpick into the center on top.
4. Once fully baked, remove the pan from the machine and let the bread remain in the pan for 5 minutes. Then, remove the bread and cool it on a wire rack.

Blueberry Bread

	Ingredients	Nutrition
2-Pound Loaf	• 1¼ cups water • 6 ounces cream cheese, softened • 2¼ tablespoons butter or margarine • ¼ cup sugar • 2¼ teaspoons salt • 4½ cups bread flour • 1⅓ teaspoon grated lemon peel • 2¼ teaspoons cardamom • 2¼ tablespoons nonfat dry milk • 2⅓ teaspoon Red Star brand active dry yeast • 2/3 cup dried blueberries	• Calories: 311 • Carbohydrate: 250 g • Fat: 3 g • Protein: 9 g • Sodium: 480 mg

Directions:

1. Combine all ingredients, excluding the dried blueberries, in the bread pan. Use the minimum amount of liquid specified in the recipe. Select the raisin/nut cycle and the light crust setting. Start the device.
2. Monitor the dough during kneading. If it appears dry or hard after 5 minutes, or if the machine struggles to knead it, gradually add more liquid, one tablespoon at a time, until the dough forms a soft, tender, slightly sticky ball.
3. Add the dried cranberries when prompted.
4. Once the bake cycle finishes, remove the bread from the pan, transfer it to a cooling rack, and let it cool.

Olive Bread with Italian Herbs

	Ingredients	Nutrition
1½ - Pound Loaf	• 1 cup (250 ml) water • ½ cup brine from olives • 4 tablespoons butter • 3¼ tablespoons sugar • 2¼ teaspoons salt • 4 cups flour • 2¼ teaspoons dry yeast • ½ cup olives • 1 teaspoon Italian herbs	• Calories: 272 • Fat: 7.5 g • Cholesterol: 15 g • Sodium: 80 mg • Carbs: 40 g • Fiber: 3 g

Directions:

1. Begin by adding all liquid ingredients to the bread maker. Then incorporate the butter.
2. Fill the bread maker with brine and water.
3. Add salt and sugar to the mixture. Gradually pour in the flour, ensuring even distribution. Sprinkle the dry yeast over the top of the flour, preferably in the corners.
4. Place the bread maker's pan into the machine and wait for the signal before the final dough kneading to add the olives and herbs.
5. While waiting, cut the olives into 2-3 parts. Once the bread maker signals, add the olives and Italian herbs into the dough.
6. Wait for the bread maker to signal that the bread is ready.
7. Once cooled, the bread should exhibit an exciting structure, along with an enticing aroma and flavor.

Orange and Walnut Bread

	Ingredients	Nutrition
1-Pound Loaf	• 1 egg white • one tablespoon water • ½ cup warm whey • one tablespoon yeast • 4 tablespoons sugar • 2 oranges, crushed • 4 cups flour • 1 teaspoon salt • 3 teaspoons orange peel • 1/3 teaspoon vanilla • 3¼ tablespoons walnut and almonds, crushed • Crushed pepper, salt, cheese for garnish	• Calories: 337 • Carbohydrates: 23 g • Total Fat: 7 g • Protein: 1½ g • Sugar: 34 g • Fiber: 1 g • Sodium: 230 mg

Directions:

1. Measure all ingredients and add them to the bread machine according to the manufacturer's instructions.
2. Select the "Dough" cycle on the bread machine and start it.
3. Once the dough cycle is complete, remove the dough from the bread machine and transfer it to a floured surface.
4. Allow the dough to rest for 5 minutes.
5. Divide the dough into thirds.
6. Roll each portion into rectangles approximately 1x5 inches in size.
7. Use a sharp knife to cut the dough into strips about ½ inch wide.

8. Take 2-3 strips and twist them together, pressing the ends together to secure.
9. Preheat the oven to 400°F (200°C).
10.   In a small bowl, whisk together the egg white and water. Brush this mixture onto the breadsticks.
11. Sprinkle sesame seeds over the breadsticks.
12. Bake until golden brown, approximately 15 minutes.

Banana-Lemon Loaf

	Ingredients	Nutrition
1 -Pound Loaf	• 2 cups all-purpose flour • ½ cup water • 1 cup bananas, very ripe and mashed • 1 cup walnuts, chopped • 1 cup of sugar • one tablespoon baking powder • 1 teaspoon lemon peel, grated • ½ teaspoon salt • 2 eggs • ½ cup of vegetable oil	• Calories: 311 • Carbohydrates: 15 g • Fat: 6 g • Protein: 3 g • Sodium: 80 mg

Directions:

1. Begin by adding bananas to the bread machine pan, followed by the wet ingredients, and then the dry ingredients.
2. Choose the "Quick" or "Cake" preset on your bread machine.
3. Allow the machine to complete its cycle.
4. Once the cycle is finished, remove the pan from the machine and let the bread cool for 5 minutes.

Australian Vegetable Bread

	Ingredients	Nutrition
1½-Pound Loaf	• 4 cups all-purpose flour • 4 tablespoons sugar • 2¼ teaspoons salt • 2¼ tablespoons olive oil • 1 teaspoon yeast • liquid (3 parts juice + 1-part water)	• Calories: 225 • Total Fat: 3.3 g • Saturated Fat: 0.5 g • Cholesterol: 0 g • Sodium: 366 mg • Carbohydrates: 40.1 g • Dietary Fiber: 1.4 g • Sugars: 4.9 g • Protein: 5.3 g •

Directions:

1. In the bread machine, knead four types of dough: three with different colors using vegetable juices (beet juice for Bordeaux, tomato juice for red, spinach juice or puree for green) and one with water for white.
2. As each type of dough is kneaded, keep the previous dough lump in a warm place to rise.
3. Use the Pasta Dough program on your bread machine.
4. Roll the finished white dough into a large sheet. Divide each colored dough into four pieces. Arrange the colored dough balls onto the white sheet, rolling them into small rolls and wrapping them in three layers in different orders to create four rolls. Enclose the colored dough completely with the white dough, shape it, and place it in the bread machine.
5. Select the baking program and set the time to 60 minutes. The goal is for the loaf to resemble plain white bread with a hidden surprise.
6. Note that the colored dough may peek out during baking.

Apple with Pumpkin Bread

	Ingredients	Nutrition
2 -Pound Loaf	• 1/3 cup dried apples, chopped • 1⅓ teaspoon bread machine yeast • 4 cups bread flour • 1/3 cup ground pecans • ⅓ teaspoon ground nutmeg • ⅓ teaspoon ground ginger • ⅓ teaspoon allspice • ½ teaspoon ground cinnamon • 3 teaspoons salt • 2¼ tablespoons unsalted butter, cubed • 1/3 cup dry skim milk powder • ¼ cup honey • 2 large eggs, at room temperature • 2/3 cup pumpkin puree • 2/3 cup water	• Calories: 318 • Carbs: 30 g • Total Fat: 4 g • Protein: 11 g • Sodium: 720 mg

Directions:

1. Combine all ingredients, except for the dried apples, in the bread pan following this order: water, pumpkin puree, eggs, honey, skim milk, butter, salt, allspice, cinnamon, pecans, nutmeg, ginger, flour, and yeast.

2. Place the pan firmly inside the bread maker and close the lid securely.
3. Place the dried apples in the fruit and nut dispenser of the bread maker.
4. Turn on the bread machine, select the sweet setting, and choose your desired crust color.
5. Once the bread is baked, carefully remove it from the machine and allow it to cool for 4-6 minutes before slicing.

Pure Peach Bread

	Ingredients	Nutrition
1½-Pound Loaf	• ¾ cup peaches, chopped • 1/3 cup heavy whipping cream • 1 egg • one tablespoon butter, melted at room temperature • 1/3 teaspoon ground cinnamon • 1½ teaspoons ground nutmeg • 2¼ tablespoons sugar • 1⅓ teaspoon salt • 1/3 cup whole-wheat flour • 2 2/3 cups white bread flour • 1 ⅓ teaspoon instant or bread machine yeast	• Calories: 201 • Carbohydrates: 11 g • Total Fat: 0.3 g • Protein: 1.1 g • Fiber: 3 g • Sodium: 230 mg •

Directions:

1. Take a 1½ pound bread pan and add the liquid ingredients first, followed by the dry ingredients.
2. Place the bread pan into the machine and securely close the lid.
3. Select the "Basic Bread/White Bread/Regular Bread" setting for the bread cycle. Choose the crust type by pressing "Light" or "Medium."
4. Start the machine, and it will begin preparing the bread.
5. Once the bread cycle is finished, open the lid and carefully remove the bread pan.
6. Allow the bread to cool for 10-15 minutes on a wire rack. Gently shake the pan to release the bread loaf.

Date Delight Bread

	Ingredients	Nutrition
1½-Pound Loaf	• ¾ cup water, lukewarm • ½ cup milk, lukewarm • 2¼ tablespoons butter, melted at room temperature • ¼ cup honey • 3¼ tablespoons molasses • one tablespoon sugar • 2¼ cups whole-wheat flour • 1¼ cups white bread flour • 2¼ tablespoons skim milk powder • 1 teaspoon salt • one tablespoon unsweetened cocoa powder • 1⅓ teaspoon instant or bread machine yeast • ¾ cup chopped dates	• Calories: 180 • Carbohydrates: 53 g • Fat 5 g • Sodium: 155 mg

Directions:

1. Start by taking a 1½ pound bread pan. Add the liquid ingredients first, then add the dry ingredients. Exclude the dates for now.

2. Place the bread pan into the machine and ensure the top lid is securely closed.

3. Plug the bread machine into a power socket. Choose a bread cycle by pressing "Basic Bread/White Bread/Regular

Bread" or "Fruit/Nut Bread," and select your desired crust type by pressing "Light" or "Medium."

4. Start the machine to begin preparing the bread. When the machine beeps or signals, add the dates.

5. After the bread cycle is completed, open the lid and remove the bread pan.

6. Allow the pan to cool for 10-15 minutes on a wire rack.

Orange Date Bread

	Ingredients	Nutrition
1-Pound Loaf	• 2 cups all-purpose flour • 1 cup dates, chopped • ¾ cup of sugar • ½ cup walnuts, chopped • 2¼ tablespoons orange rind, grated • 1⅓ teaspoon baking powder • 1 teaspoon baking soda • ½ cup of orange juice • ½ cup of water • 1 pinch salt • one tablespoon vegetable oil • 1 teaspoon vanilla extract	• Calories: 180 • Carbohydrates: 1 g • Fat: 3 g • Protein: 1 g • Sodium: 20 mg

Directions:

1. Begin by adding the wet ingredients followed by the dry ingredients into the bread pan.
2. Select the "Quick" or "Cake" mode on your bread machine.
3. Allow the machine to complete all cycles.
4. Once the cycle is finished, remove the pan from the machine, but keep the bread in the pan for an additional 5 minutes.
5. After 5 minutes, carefully remove the bread from the pan and allow it to cool completely before slicing.

Zero-Fat Carrot Pineapple Loaf

	Ingredients	Nutrition
1-Pound Loaf	• 2½ cups all-purpose flour • ¾ cup of sugar • ½ cup pineapples, crushed • ½ cup carrots, grated • ½ cup raisins • 2¼ teaspoons baking powder • ½ teaspoon ground cinnamon • ½ teaspoon salt • ⅓ teaspoon allspice • ⅓ teaspoon nutmeg • ½ cup applesauce • one tablespoon molasses	• Calories: 180 • Carbohydrates: 1 g • Fat: 0 g • Protein: 1 g • Sodium: 80 mg

Directions:

1. Begin by adding the wet ingredients to the bread pan before adding the dry ingredients.
2. Select the "Quick" or "Cake" mode on your bread machine.
3. Allow the machine to complete all cycles.
4. Once the cycle is finished, remove the pan from the machine, but wait an additional 5 minutes before transferring the bread to a wire rack.
5. Allow the bread to cool completely before slicing.

Autumn Treasures Loaf

	Ingredients	Nutrition
1-Pound Loaf	• 1 cup all-purpose flour • ½ cup dried fruit, chopped • ¼ cup pecans, chopped • ¼ cup of sugar • 2¼ tablespoons baking powder • 1 teaspoon salt • ⅓ teaspoon of baking soda • ½ teaspoon ground nutmeg • 1 cup apple juice • ¼ cup of vegetable oil • 3¼ tablespoons aquafaba • 1 teaspoon of vanilla extract	• Calories: 180 • Carbohydrates: 1½ g • Fat: 3 g • Sodium: 230 mg • Protein: 1 g

Directions:

1. Begin by adding all wet ingredients to the bread pan before adding the dry ingredients.
2. Turn on the bread machine using the "Quick" or "Cake" setting.
3. Wait for the machine to complete all cycles.
4. Once the cycle is finished, remove the bread pan from the machine.
5. After 5 minutes, carefully transfer the bread from the pan to a wire rack.
6. Allow the bread to cool completely before slicing.

Oatmeal Walnut Bread

	Ingredients	Nutrition
1-Pound Loaf	• ¾ cup whole-wheat flour • ¼ cup all-purpose flour • ½ cup brown sugar • 1/3 cup walnuts, chopped • ¼ cup oatmeal • ⅓ teaspoon of baking soda • 2¼ tablespoons baking powder • 1 teaspoon salt • 1 cup Vegan buttermilk • ¼ cup of vegetable oil • 3¼ tablespoons aquafaba	• Calories: 220 • Carbohydrates: 11 g • Fat: 3 g • Sodium: 155 mg • Protein: 3 g •

Directions:

1. Begin by adding the wet ingredients to the bread pan, followed by the dry ingredients.
2. Select the "Quick" or "Cake" setting on your bread machine.
3. Allow the machine to complete all cycles.
4. Once the cycle is finished, remove the pan from the machine.
5. Allow the bread to sit in the pan for 5 minutes.
6. After 5 minutes, carefully remove the bread from the pan.
7. Slice and serve the bread after it has cooled.

Pumpkin Raisin Bread

	Ingredients	Nutrition
1-Pound Loaf	• ½ cup all-purpose flour • ½ cup whole-wheat flour • ½ cup pumpkin, mashed • ½ cup raisins • ¼ cup brown sugar • 2¼ tablespoons baking powder • 1 teaspoon salt • 1 teaspoon pumpkin pie spice • ⅓ teaspoon baking soda • ¾ cup apple juice • ¼ cup of vegetable oil • 3¼ tablespoons aquafaba	• •Calories: 180 • •Carbohydrates: 1½ • •Fat: 3 g • •Protein: 1 g • •Sodium: 230 mg

Directions:

1. Arrange the ingredients in the bread pan in this order: oil, pumpkin, sugar, flour, baking soda, baking powder, raisins, pumpkin pie spice, and aquafaba.
2. Select the "Quick" or "Cake" mode on your bread machine.
3. Allow the machine to complete all cycles.
4. After the cycle is complete, remove the pan from the machine. Let the bread sit in the pan for 5 minutes.
5. Transfer the bread to a wire rack to cool completely before slicing.

Hawaiian Bread

	Ingredients	Nutrition
1-Pound Loaf	• 3 cups bread flour • 2½ tablespoons brown sugar • ¾ teaspoon salt • 2¼ teaspoons quick-rising yeast • 1 egg • ¾ cup pineapple juice • 2¼ tablespoons almond milk • 2¼ tablespoons vegetable oil	• Calories: 190 • Carbohydrates: 30 g • Fat: 3 g • Protein: 4 g

Directions:

1. Combine all the wet ingredients thoroughly in the bread pan.
2. Select a light crust color and choose the "Basic" or "Normal" setting on your bread maker.
3. Allow the machine to complete the cycles of mixing, kneading, and baking.
4. Once the cycle is finished, remove the pan from the machine.
5. Place the freshly baked bread on a cooling wire rack.
6. Allow the bread to cool for about an hour before slicing and serving.

Black Forest Loaf

	Ingredients	Nutrition
1-Pound Loaf	• 1½ cups bread flour • 1 cup whole wheat flour • 1 cup rye flour • 3¼ tablespoons cocoa • one tablespoon caraway seeds • 2¼ teaspoons yeast • 1⅓ teaspoon salt • 1¼ cups water • 1/3 cup molasses • 1⅓ tablespoons canola oil	• Calories: 176 • Carbohydrates: 27 g • Sodium: 360 mg • Fat: 3 g • Protein: 3 g

Directions:

1. Start by combining all ingredients in the bread pan, beginning with the wet ingredients and then adding the dry ones.
2. Select the "Normal" or "Basic" mode on your bread machine, and choose a light crust color setting.
3. Once the cycle is complete, remove the bread from the machine.
4. Allow the bread to cool completely before slicing and serving.

Vegan Cinnamon Raisin Bread

	Ingredients	Nutrition
1-Pound Loaf	• 2¼ cups oat flour • ¾ cup raisins • ½ cup almond flour • ¼ cup of coconut sugar • 2⅓ teaspoon cinnamon • 1 teaspoon baking powder • ½ teaspoon baking soda • ⅓ teaspoon salt • ¾ cup of water • ½ cup of soy milk • ¼ cup maple syrup • 3¼ tablespoons coconut oil • 1 teaspoon vanilla extract	• Calories: 190 • Carbohydrates: 26 g • Fat: 3 g • Protein: 3 g • Sodium: 60 mg

Directions:

1. Start by filling the bread pan with all of the wet ingredients first, followed by the dry ingredients.
2. Select the "Cake" or "Quick" setting on your bread maker.
3. Allow the machine to complete the cycles of mixing and baking.
4. Once the cycles are finished, carefully remove the pan from the machine.
5. Let the bread rest in the pan for an additional five minutes.
6. Transfer the bread to a wire rack to cool completely.
7. Slice and serve the bread after it has cooled.

Beer Bread

	Ingredients	Nutrition
1-Pound Loaf	• 3 cups bread flour • 2¼ tablespoons sugar • 2⅓ teaspoons yeast • 1⅓ teaspoon salt • 2/3 cup beer • 1/3 cup water • 2¼ tablespoons vegetable oil	• Calories: 180 • Carbohydrates: 25 g • Fat: 1 g • Protein: 4 g • Sodium: 230 mg

Directions:

1. Fill the bread pan with water, beer, oil, salt, sugar, flour, and yeast, in that sequence.
2. Turn on the bread maker using the "Basic" or "Normal" mode and adjust the crust color to light to medium.
3. Allow the machine to complete all cycles.
4. Once the cycle is finished, remove the pan from the machine.
5. Transfer the beer bread onto a wire rack and allow it to cool for about an hour.
6. After cooling, slice the bread into 1½-pound portions and serve.

Onion and Mushroom Bread

	Ingredients	Nutrition
1 -Pound Loaf	• 4 ounces mushrooms, chopped • 4 cups bread flour • 3¼ tablespoons sugar • 4 teaspoons fast-acting yeast • 4 teaspoons dried onions, minced • 1⅓ teaspoon salt • ½ teaspoon garlic powder • ¾ cup of water	• Calories: 151 • Carbohydrates: 25 g • Fat: 0 g • Protein: 5 g

Directions:

1. Start by pouring water into the bread pan, followed by adding all the dry ingredients.
2. Set the bread machine to the "Fast" cycle mode.
3. Allow the machine to complete all cycles.
4. Once the cycle is done, remove the bread from the pan and transfer it onto a wire rack.
5. Let the bread cool for one hour before slicing it into 1½-inch pieces.

Low-Carb Multigrain Bread

	Ingredients	Nutrition
1 -Pound Loaf	• ¾ cup whole-wheat flour • ¼ cup cornmeal • ¼ cup oatmeal • 2¼ tablespoons 7-grain cereals • 2¼ tablespoons baking powder • 1 teaspoon salt • ⅓ teaspoon baking soda • ¾ cup of water • ¼ cup of vegetable oil • ¼ cup of orange juice • 3¼ tablespoons aquafaba	• Carbohydrates: 9 g • •Fat: 3 g • •Protein: 1 g • •Sodium: 230 mg • •Calories: 175

Directions:

1. Begin by adding the wet ingredients to the bread pan, followed by the dry ingredients.
2. Choose the "Cake" or "Quick" setting on your bread maker.
3. Allow the machine to complete all cycles.
4. Once the cycle is finished, remove the bread pan from the machine.
5. Let the bread rest in the pan for 5 minutes before transferring it to cool further on a wire rack.
6. After cooling for an hour, slice the bread and serve.

Mashed Potato Bread

	Ingredients	Nutrition
1 -Pound Loaf	• 2 1/3 cups bread flour • ½ cup mashed potatoes • one tablespoon sugar • 1 ⅓ teaspoon yeast • ¾ teaspoon salt • ¼ cup potato water • one tablespoon ground flax seeds • 4 teaspoons oil	• Calories: 180 • Carbohydrates: 26 g • Fiber: 3 g • Sodium: 180 mg

Directions:

1. Add the potato water, oil, flax seeds, mashed potatoes, sugar, salt, flour, and yeast to the bread pan in that sequence.
2. Set the bread machine to the "Basic" or "Normal" mode and choose a medium crust color setting.
3. Allow the bread machine to complete all cycles.
4. Once the cycle is finished, carefully remove the bread pan from the machine.
5. Take the bread out of the pan and place it on a wire rack to cool.
6. Let the bread cool completely before slicing and serving.

Cakes and Quick Bread

Honey Pound Cake

	Ingredients	Nutrition
1-Pound Loaf	• 1 cup butter, unsalted • ½ cup water • ¼ cup honey • 2¼ tablespoons whole milk • 4 eggs, beaten • 1 cup of sugar • 2 cups flour • Pinch of salt	• Calories: 187 • Sodium: 33 mg • Dietary Fiber: 0.3 g • Fat: 6.9 g • Carbohydrates: 13 g • Protein: 1.7 g

Directions:

1. Allow the butter to soften to room temperature and cut it into ½-inch cubes.
2. Place all ingredients into the bread machine in the specified order: butter, honey, milk, eggs, sugar, flour.
3. Select the Sweetbread setting, choose a light crust color, then press Start.
4. Once finished, remove the bread from the bread pan using a rubber spatula.
5. Cool on a rack and serve with your favorite fruit.

Carrot Cake Bread

	Ingredients	Nutrition
1-Pound Loaf	• Non-stick cooking spray • ¼ cup vegetable oil • 2 large eggs, room temperature • ½ teaspoon pure vanilla extract • ½ cup sugar • ¼ cup light brown sugar • ¼ cup of crushed pineapple with juice (from a can or fresh) • 5 cups unbleached, all-purpose flour • 1 teaspoon baking powder • ⅓ teaspoon baking soda • ⅓ teaspoon salt • 1 teaspoon ground cloves • ¾ teaspoon ground cinnamon • 1 cup freshly grated carrots • 1/3 cup chopped pecans • 1/3 cup golden raisins	• Calories: 181 • Sodium: 60 mg • Protein: 2,4g • Dietary Fiber: 1.3 g • Fat: 7.3 g • Carbs: 11 g

Directions:

1. Spray the inside of the bread pan with non-stick cooking spray.
2. Put all the ingredients into the bread pan in the listed order.
3. Select the Express Bake setting, choose medium crust color, and press Start. During mixing, use a rubber spatula to scrape the sides of the bread pan to ensure all ingredients are fully incorporated.

4.Once baked, remove the bread from the pan and let it cool completely on a wire rack before slicing and serving

Lemon Cake

	Ingredients	Nutrition
1 ½-Pound Loaf	• large eggs, beaten • 1/3 cup milk • ½ cup butter, melted • 2 cups all-purpose flour • 3 teaspoons baking powder • 1 1/3 cups sugar • 1 teaspoon vanilla extract • 2 lemons, zested • For the glaze: • 1 cup powdered sugar • 2¼ tablespoons lemon juice, freshly squeezed	• Calories: 290 • Sodium: 77 mg • Dietary Fiber: 0.6 g • Fat: 9.3 g • Carbohydrates: 42.9 g • Protein: 4 g. •

Directions:

1. Mix the powdered sugar and lemon juice in a small bowl to prepare the glaze, then set aside.
2. Place all remaining ingredients into the baking pan following the order listed.
3. Choose the Sweetbread setting, select medium crust color, and press Start.
4. Once baked, transfer the baking pan to a cooling rack.
5. After the cake has cooled, gently remove it onto a serving plate. Glaze the cooled cake and serve.

Chocolate Marble Cake

	Ingredients	Nutrition
1½-Pounds Loaf	• 1½ cups water • 1⅓ teaspoon vanilla extract • 1⅓ teaspoon salt • 3½ cups bread flour • 1⅓ teaspoon instant yeast • 1 cup semi-sweet chocolate chips	• Calories: 202 • Sodium: 241 mg • Dietary Fiber: 1.6 g • Fat: 4.3 g • Carbohydrates: 30.1 g • Protein: 3 g •

Directions:

1. Reserve the chocolate chips and add the remaining ingredients to the bread maker's pan.
2. Set the machine to Sweetbread mode and start the process by pressing Start.
3. Check the dough after 15 minutes of kneading to ensure it forms a smooth ball, remaining soft without being sticky.
4. Add the chocolate chips approximately 3 minutes before the second kneading cycle is complete.
5. Once fully baked, use a rubber spatula to remove the loaf and allow it to cool on a rack before serving.

Pumpkin Spice Cake

	Ingredients	Nutrition
1½-Pounds Loaf	<ul><li>1 cup of sugar</li><li>1 cup canned pumpkin</li><li>1/3 cup vegetable oil</li><li>1 teaspoon vanilla extract</li><li>2 eggs</li><li>1 ½ cups all-purpose flour</li><li>2¼ teaspoons baking powder</li><li>⅓ teaspoon salt</li><li>1 teaspoon ground cinnamon</li><li>⅓ teaspoon ground nutmeg</li><li>1⅓ teaspoon ground cloves</li><li>Shortening, for greasing pan</li></ul>	<ul><li>Calories: 230</li><li>Dietary Fiber: 1.3 g</li><li>Fat: 7.1 g</li><li>Carbs: 31.3 g</li><li>Protein: 2.1 g</li><li>Sodium: 46 mg</li></ul>

Directions:

1. Grease the bread maker pan and kneading blade generously with shortening.
2. Add all ingredients into the pan following the specified order.
3. Select the Rapid cycle and start the process by pressing Start.
4. Three minutes into the cycle, open the lid.
5. Use a rubber spatula to carefully scrape down the sides of the pan, then close the lid to resume the cycle.
6. Allow the baked cake to cool on a wire rack for 5 minutes before slicing.

Lemon Blueberry Quick Bread

	Ingredients	Nutrition
-	• 2 cups all-purpose flour • 1⅓ teaspoon baking powder • ½ teaspoon salt • one tablespoon lemon zest • 1 cup of sugar • ½ cup unsalted butter, softened • 2 large eggs • 2¼ teaspoons pure vanilla extract • ½ cup whole milk • 1½ cups blueberries For the crumb topping: • 1/3 cup sugar • 3¼ tablespoons all-purpose flour • 2¼ tablespoons butter, melted • Non-stick cooking spray	• Calories: 462 • Sodium: 120 mg • Dietary Fiber: 1 g • Fat: 32.1 g • Carbohydrates: 41.1 g • Protein: 4 g

Directions:

1. Apply non-stick cooking spray to the bread maker pan and lightly dust with flour.
2. Prepare the crumb topping ingredients and set them aside.
3. In a small bowl, whisk together flour, baking powder, and salt; set aside.

4. In a large bowl, combine sugar and lemon zest, mixing thoroughly. Incorporate butter and beat until light and fluffy. Add eggs, vanilla, and milk; mix well.

5. Blend in the flour mixture until fully combined. Fold in blueberries and evenly spread the batter into the bread maker pan.

6. Sprinkle the prepared crumb topping over the batter. Choose the Sweetbread setting, select a light crust color, and start the cycle.

7. Once the cake is baked, allow it to cool on a wire rack for 15 minutes before serving warm.

Apricot almond bread

	Ingredients	Nutrition
2-Pound Loaf	• 1 cup butter, unsalted • 1 cup of sugar • 2 eggs • 1 cup sour cream • 1 teaspoon vanilla extract • 2 cups all-purpose flour • 1 teaspoon baking powder • 1 teaspoon baking soda • ½ teaspoon salt	• Calories 139.2 • Total Fat 4.1 g • Saturated Fat 1.0 g • Polyunsaturated Fat 0.7 g • Monounsaturated Fat 2.0 g • Cholesterol 15.4 mg • Sodium 129.3 mg • Potassium 161.9 mg • Total Carbohydrate 26.0 g • Dietary Fiber 2.3 g • Sugars 12.9 g • Protein 3.5 g

Directions:

1. Measure all ingredients into the bread machine pan following the order suggested by the manufacturer, incorporating apricots and nuts with the flour.
2. Process the mixture in the basic/white bread cycle, selecting either a light or medium/normal color crust setting depending on your machine's baking tendencies.
3. After the baking cycle, avoid opening the bread machine immediately; allow the bread to rest for a few minutes to ensure a better texture.
4. Carefully remove the baked bread from the pan and transfer it to a wire rack for thorough cooling.
5. To enhance the flavor, consider experimenting with different types of nuts or adding a touch of cinnamon or vanilla extract to the dough.

Cinnamon Pecan Coffee Cake

	Ingredients	Nutrition
2-Pound Loaf	• 1 cup butter, unsalted • 1 cup of sugar • 2 eggs • 1 cup sour cream • 1 teaspoon vanilla extract • 2 cups all-purpose flour • 1 teaspoon baking powder • 1 teaspoon baking soda • ½ teaspoon salt	• Calories: 411 • Carbohydrates: 10 g • Sodium: 120 mg • Fiber: 2.5 g • Fat: 32.1 g

Directions:

1. Place butter, sugar, eggs, sour cream, and vanilla into the bread maker baking pan, followed by the dry ingredients.
2. Choose the Cake cycle and start by pressing Start. Prepare toppings and set them aside.
3. After the kneading cycle is complete (approximately 1 minute), sprinkle 1/2 cup of topping over the dough and resume baking.
4. In the final hour of baking, sprinkle the remaining 1/2 cup of topping onto the cake. Bake until fully done.
5. Allow the cake to cool on a wire rack for 5 minutes before serving while still warm.

Pleasure Bread

Crisp White Bread

	Ingredients	Nutrition
1-Pound Loaf	• ¾ cup lukewarm water • one tablespoon butter, melted • one tablespoon white sugar • ¾ teaspoon sea salt • 2¼ tablespoons of milk powder • 2 cups wheat flour • ¾ teaspoon active dry yeast	• Calories: 183 • Total Fat: 1.4 g • Saturated Fat: 0.1 g • Cholesterol: 3 g • Sodium: 181 mg • Carbohydrates: 18.6 g • Dietary Fiber: 0.7 g • Sugars: 2.1 g • Protein: 3.3 g • Calcium: 24 mg • Potassium: 33 mg •

Directions:

1. Gather all the ingredients for your bread and the measuring tools (cup, spoon, kitchen scales).
2. Accurately measure the ingredients into the pan.
3. Place all the ingredients into the bread bucket in the correct sequence, following your bread machine's manual.
4. Secure the lid. Set the bread machine to the "BASIC"/"WHITE BREAD" program and select "MEDIUM" for the crust color.
5. Press START and wait for the program to finish.
6. Once done, remove the bucket and let it cool for 5 minutes.
7. Remove the loaf from the pan and let it cool on a cooling rack for 30 minutes.

Mediterranean Semolina Bread

	Ingredients	Nutrition
1½-Pound Loaf	• 1 cup lukewarm water • 1 teaspoon salt • 2½ tablespoons butter, melted • 2⅓ teaspoon white sugar • 2¼ cups all-purpose flour • 1/3 cup semolina • 1⅓ teaspoon active dry yeast	• Calories: 230 • Total Fat: 1.1 g • Saturated Fat: 4.9 g • Cholesterol: 1 g • Sodium: 230 mg • Carbohydrates: 37 g • Dietary Fiber: 1.5 g • Total Sugars: 2.1 g • Protein: 5.3 g • Calcium: 1¼ mg • Potassium: 1 mg •

Directions:

1. Gather all the ingredients for your bread and the measuring tools (cup, spoon, kitchen scales).
2. Accurately measure the ingredients into the pan.
3. Place all the ingredients into the bread bucket in the correct order, following your bread machine's manual.
4. Close the cover.
5. Set your bread machine to the Italian Bread/Sandwich program and choose "Medium" for the crust color.
6. Press START and wait for the program to finish.
7. When done, remove the bucket and let it cool for 5 minutes.
8. Remove the loaf from the pan and let it cool on a cooling rack for 30 minutes.

Mustard Sour Cream Bread

	Ingredients	Nutrition
2-Pound Loaf	• 1¼ cups lukewarm milk • 3¼ tablespoons sunflower oil • 3¼ tablespoons sour cream • 2¼ tablespoons dry mustard • 1 egg • ½ sachet sugar vanilla • 4 cups wheat flour • 1 teaspoon active dry yeast • 2¼ tablespoons white sugar • 2¼ teaspoons sea salt	• Calories: 340 • Total Fat: 9.3 g • Saturated Fat: 1.7 g • Cholesterol: 26 g • Sodium: 471 mg • Carbohydrates: 54.6 g • Dietary Fiber: 2.3 g • Sugars: 5.5 g • Protein: 9.3

Directions:

1. Compile the ingredients for your bread as well as the measurement equipment (cup, spoon, and kitchen scales).
2. Evenly weigh the components into the pan.
3. According to the Directions: in your bread machine manual, add all the ingredients to the bread bucket in the correct order.
4. Put the lid on the bucket. Select "MEDIUM" for the crust color and set your bread machine to the "BASIC" program.
5. Press the START button and let the program finish.
6. After it's done, take out the bucket and let it cool for five minutes.
7. Remove the loaf from the pan by giving it a shake, then let it cool on a cooling rack for 30 minutes.

Honey Rye Bread

	Ingredients	Nutrition
1½-Pound Loaf	• 2¼ cups wheat flour • ¼ cup rye flour • 1 cup 10 ml lukewarm water • 1 egg • one tablespoon olive oil • 1 teaspoon salt • 1⅓ tablespoons liquid honey • 1 teaspoon active dry yeast	• Calories: 177 • Total Fat: 2.7 g • Sat Fat: 0.6 g • Cholesterol: 1 g • Sodium: 230 mg • Carbohydrates: 33.1 g • Dietary Fiber: 2.0 g • Protein: 5.1 • Sugars: 3.4 g •

Directions:

1. Compile the ingredients for your bread as well as the measurement equipment (cup, spoon, and kitchen scales).
2. Evenly weigh the components into the pan.
3. Fill the bread bucket with all the ingredients in the appropriate sequence, following the Directions: in the bread machine's handbook.
4. Shut the lid. On your bread machine, select the "BASIC" program and choose either "MEDIUM" or DARK for the crust color.
5. Press the START button and let the program finish.
6. Once done, take out the bucket and let it cool for five minutes.
7. Remove the loaf from the pan by giving it a shake, then let it cool on a cooling rack for 30 minutes.

Tomato Paprika Bread

	Ingredients	Nutrition
1½-Pounds Loaf	• 1⅓ teaspoon active dry yeast • 3 cups bread flour • 2¼ tablespoons white sugar • 1 teaspoon salt • 1⅓ tablespoons butter, melted • 1 cup lukewarm water • 2¼ teaspoons ground paprika • 1 cup dried tomatoes, chopped	• Calories: 183 • Total Fat: 4.3 g • Saturated Fat: 2.6 g • Cholesterol: 1¼ g • Sodium: 230 mg • Carbohydrates: 10.5 g • Dietary Fiber: 1.3 g • Protein: 3.1g • Sugars: 1.7 g • Calcium: 7 mg • Potassium:17 mg

Directions:

1. Gather all of your bread ingredients and measurement tools (a cup, a spoon, and kitchen scales).
2. Carefully measure everything into the pan, omitting the tomatoes.
3. Arrange all the ingredients in the correct sequence in the bread bucket, as directed by the bread machine's handbook.
4. Shut the lid.
5. Choose "MEDIUM" or DARK for the crust color and set your bread maker to the "BASIC" program.
6. Hit the START button. Once the signal is given, add the diced tomatoes to the dough.
7. Wait until the program finishes.
8. After it finishes, remove the bucket and allow it to cool for five minutes.
9. Shake the loaf out of the pan and place it on a cooling rack to cool for 30 minutes.

Bran Bread

	Ingredients	Nutrition
1-Pound Loaf	• 2½ cups all-purpose flour, sifted • 1 whole egg • ¾ cup bran • 1 cup lukewarm water • one tablespoon sunflower oil • 2¼ teaspoons brown sugar • 1 teaspoon sea salt • 1 teaspoon active dry yeast	• Calories: 307 • Total Fat: 5.1 g • Sat Fat: 0.9 g • Protein: 1 ¼ g • Cholesterol: 33 g • Sodium: 230 mg • Carbs: 54 g • Dietary Fiber: 7.9 g • Total Sugars: 1.1 g

Directions:

1. Gather all the necessary ingredients for your bread and your measuring tools (a cup, a spoon, kitchen scales).
2. Carefully measure the ingredients into the pan.
3. Place all the ingredients into the bread bucket in the correct order, referring to your bread machine manual.
4. Close the lid. Set your bread machine to the "FRENCH BREAD" program and choose "MEDIUM" for the crust color.
5. Press START.
6. Allow the program to run until it finishes.
7. Once done, remove the bucket and let it cool for 5 minutes.

Honey Beer Bread

	Ingredients	Nutrition
1½-Pound Loaf	• 1/6 cups light beer, without foam • 2¼ tablespoons of liquid honey • one tablespoon olive oil • 1 teaspoon sea salt • 1 teaspoon cumin • 2¾ cups bread flour • 1⅓ teaspoon active dry yeast	• Cal: 180 • Sodium: 230 mg • Total Fat 1.6 g • Sat Fat: 0.3 gCholesterol: 0 g Carbs: 42.3 g • Dietary Fiber: 1.1 g T. • Sugars: 2.6 g • Protein: 6 g • Calcium: 1¼ mg • Potassium: 91 mg •

Directions:

1. Assemble all the necessary ingredients for your bread and your measuring tools (a cup, a spoon, kitchen scales).
2. Accurately measure the ingredients into the pan.
3. Add all the ingredients into the bread bucket in the correct order, following your bread machine manual.
4. Secure the lid. Set your bread machine to the "BASIC" program and select "MEDIUM" for the crust color.
5. Press START and wait for the program to finish.
6. Once completed, remove the bucket and let it cool for 5 minutes.
7. Shake the loaf out of the pan and let it cool on a cooling rack for 30 minutes.
8. Slice, serve, and enjoy your freshly baked bread.

Egg Bread

	Ingredients	Nutrition
1½-Pound Loaf	• 4 cups bread flour, sifted • 1 cup lukewarm milk • 2 whole eggs • 1 teaspoon active dry yeast • 1⅓ teaspoon salt • 2¼ tablespoons white sugar • 1⅓ tablespoons butter, melted •	• Calories: 319 • Fat: 5.6 g • Cholesterol: 56 g • Sodium: 365 mg • Carbohydrates: 56.7 g • Fiber: 1.1 g

Directions:

1. Gather all the ingredients for your bread as well as your measuring tools (cup, spoon, and kitchen scales).
2. Gently weigh the components into the pan.
3. Follow the Directions: in your bread machine's handbook and add all the ingredients to the bread bucket in the correct order.
4. Snap the lid shut. Choose "MEDIUM" for the crust color and set your bread maker to the "BASIC" program.
5. Press the START button and wait for the program to finish.
6. After it finishes, remove the bucket and let it cool for five minutes.
7. Shake the loaf out of the pan and let it rest on a cooling rack for 30 minutes.
8. Cut, serve, and savor the flavor of aromatic, freshly baked bread.

Whole-Wheat Bread

Whole Wheat Bread

	1-Pound	1 ½-Pound	2-Pound	Nutrition
Lukewarm whole milk	½ cup	1 cup	11/3 cups	• Calories: 231
Unsalted butter, diced	2¼ tablespoons	3¼ tablespoons	4 tablespoons	• Total fat: 3.3 g
Whole wheat flour	1 cup	1½ cups	2 cups	• Sat fat: 1.1½ g • Cholesterol: 1½ mg
Plain bread flour	1 cup	1½ cups	2 cups	• Carbohydrates: 22.9 g
Brown sugar	2 ½ tablespoons	3 one tablespoons	5 tablespoons	• Dietary fiber: 2.1 g
Salt	¾ teaspoon	1⅓ teaspoons	1⅓ teaspoon	• Sodium: 139 mg
Bread machine yeast	¾ teaspoon	1⅓ teaspoons	1⅓ teaspoon	• Protein: 3.9 g

Directions:

1. Place the ingredients into the bread machine following the order listed above, or consult your bread machine's instruction manual for guidance.
2. Choose the whole wheat setting and select medium crust.
3. Once baked, transfer the bread onto a cooling rack to cool, then serve.

Whole Wheat and Honey Bread

	1-Pound	1½-Pound	2-Pound	Nutrition
Lukewarm water	1 cup	1½ cups	2¼ cups	• Calories: 180
Honey	3¼ tablespoons	4½ tablespoons	6 tablespoons	• Total fat: 3.5 g • Saturated fat: 0 g
Vegetable oil	2¼ tablespoons	3¼ tablespoons	4 tablespoons	• Cholesterol: 0 mg
Plain bread flour	1½ cup	2 ¼ cups	3 cups	• Total carbohydrates : 33.4 g
Whole wheat flour	1½ cups	2 ¼ cups	3 cups	• Dietary fiber: 2.1 ½ g
Salt	1/3 teaspoon	⅓ teaspoon	½ teaspoon	• Sodium: 79 mg
Instant dry yeast	1⅓ teaspoon	2⅓ teaspoons	3 teaspoons	• Protein: 5.3 g

Directions:

1. Place the ingredients into the bread machine following the order listed above, or consult your bread machine's instruction manual.
2. Select the whole wheat setting and choose medium crust.
3. Once the bread is baked, transfer it onto a cooling rack and let it cool before serving.

Whole Wheat Bread

	1-Pound	1 ½-Pound	2-Pound	Nutrition
Lukewarm water	1 cup	1 ½ cups	2 cups	• Calories: 229
Milk powder	1¼ tablespoons	2¼ tablespoons	2½ tablespoons	• Total fat: 1 g • Saturated fat: 0.5 g
Unsalted butter, diced	one tablespoon	1⅓ tablespoons	2½ tablespoons	• Cholesterol: 1.7 mg
Honey	one tablespoon	1⅓ tablespoons	2½ tablespoons	• Carbohydrates: 30.4 g • Dietary fiber: 0.9 g
Molasses	1 tablespoon	2¼ tablespoons	2½ tablespoons	• Sodium: 155 mg
Salt	1 teaspoon	1⅓ teaspoon	2¼ teaspoons	• Protein: 4.0 g
Whole wheat flour	2¼ cups	31/3 cups	4½ cups	

Directions:

1. Place the ingredients into the bread machine following the order listed above, or consult your bread machine's instruction manual.
2. Select the whole wheat setting and choose medium crust.
3. Once the bread is baked, remove it from the bread machine and transfer it onto a cooling rack to cool before serving.

Seeded Whole Wheat Bread

	1-Pound	1½-Pound	2-Pound	Nutrition
Lukewarm water	2/3cup	1 cup	¼ cups	• Calories: 230 • Total fat: 3 g • Saturated fat: 1 g • Cholesterol: 2 mg • Carbohydrates: 1 g • Dietary fiber: 1 g • Sodium: 133 mg • Protein: 3 g
Milk powder	3¼ tablespoons	4½ tablespoons	6 tablespoons	
Honey	one tablespoon	1⅓ tablespoons	2¼ tablespoons	
Unsalted butter, softened	one tablespoon	1⅓ tablespoons	2¼ tablespoons	
Plain bread flour	1 cup	1½ cups	2 cups	
Whole wheat flour	1 cup	1½ cups	2 cups	
Poppy seeds	2¼ tablespoons	3¼ tablespoons	4 tablespoons	

Directions:
1. Place the ingredients into the bread machine in the order specified above, or as instructed in your bread machine's manual.
2. Choose the Basic setting and select the medium crust option.
3. Once the bread is baked, remove it from the machine, place it on a cooling rack, and let it cool before serving.

Meat Bread

French Ham Bread

	Ingredients	Nutrition
1½-Pound Loaf	• 3 1/3 cups wheat flour • 1 cup ham • ½ cup of milk powder • 1⅓ tablespoons sugar • 1 teaspoon yeast, fresh • 1 teaspoon salt • 1 teaspoon dried basil • 1 1/3 cups water • 2¼ tablespoons olive oil	• Calories: 180 • Total Fat: 5.5g • Sat Fat: 1.1 g • Cholesterol: 1g • Sodium: 230 mg • Carbs: 47.3 g • Dietary Fiber: 1.7 g • Sugars: 6.4 g • Protein: 11.4 g •

Directions:

1. Cut the ham into 1 cm pieces.
2. Fill the bread machine with the following ingredients: water, yeast, sugar, milk powder, ham, olive oil, salt, and flour.
3. Add the ingredients as directed by the manual for your bread maker.
4. Add basil at the signal or place it in the dispenser.
5. Turn on the bread maker.
6. After the baking cycle is complete, let the bread rest in the bread machine for an hour.

Meat Bread

	Ingredients	Nutrition
1½-Pound Loaf	• 2 cups boiled chicken • 1 cup milk • 3 cups flour • one tablespoon dry yeast • 1 egg • 1¼ teaspoon sugar • ½ tablespoon salt • 2¼ tablespoons oil	• Calories: 180 • Total Fat: 6.3 g • Saturated Fat: 1.4 g • Cholesterol: 50 g • Sodium: 120 mg • Carbohydrates: 31 g • Dietary Fiber: 1.6 g • Sugars: 3 g • Protein: 17.3 g

Directions:

1. First, precook the meat using a leg or fillet.
2. Remove the meat from the bone and cut it into small pieces.
3. Fill the bread maker with all the ingredients as directed.
4. Add the chicken pieces at this stage.
5. Choose the Basic cycle.

Fish Bell Pepper Bran Bread

	Ingredients	Nutrition
1½-Pound Loaf	• 2½ cups flour • ½ cup bran • 1 1/3 cups water • 1⅓ teaspoon salt • 1⅓ teaspoon sugar • 1⅓ tablespoons mustard oil • 1⅓ teaspoons dry yeast • 2¼ teaspoons powdered milk • 1 cup chopped bell pepper • ¾ cup chopped smoked fish • 1 onion	• Calories: 180 • Total Fat 3.1 ½ g • Saturated Fat: 0.5 g • Cholesterol: 1 ½ g • Sodium: 411mg • Carbohydrates: 36 g • Dietary Fiber: 4.3 g • Sugars: 2.7 g • Protein: 7.3 g

Directions:

1. Finely chop the onion and sauté until golden brown.
2. Dice the fish into small pieces and chop the pepper into cubes.
3. Place all the ingredients into the bread machine pan.
4. Set the bread machine to the appropriate baking program.

Sausage Bread

	Ingredients	Nutrition
1 ½-Pound Loaf	• 1⅓ teaspoon dry yeast • 3 cups flour • 1¼ teaspoon sugar • 1⅓ teaspoon salt • 1 1/3 cups whey • one tablespoon oil • 1 cup chopped smoked sausage	• Calories: 234 • Total Fat 5.1 g • Saturated Fat: 1.3 g • Cholesterol: 9 g • Sodium: 405 mg • Carbohydrates: 31 g • Dietary Fiber: 1.4 g • Sugars: 2.7 g • Protein: 7.4 g

Directions:

1. Add all the ingredients in the order recommended by your bread machine's manual.
2. Select the appropriate baking settings for bread.
3. Once the bread is finished baking, remove it from the bread machine.
4. Allow the freshly baked bread to cool down before enjoying it with sausage.

Cheese Sausage Bread

	Ingredients	Nutrition
1 ½-Pound Loaf	• 1 teaspoon dry yeast • 3½ cups flour • 1 teaspoon salt • one tablespoon sugar • 1⅓ tablespoons oil • 2¼ tablespoons smoked sausage • 2¼ tablespoons grated cheese • one tablespoon chopped garlic • 1 cup of water	• Calories: 260 • Total Fat 5.6 g • Saturated Fat: 1.4 g • Cholesterol: 1½ g • Sodium: 355 mg • Carbohydrates: 40 g • Dietary Fiber: 1.6 g • Sugars: 1.7 g • Protein: 7.7 g •

Directions:

1. Cut the sausage into small pieces.
2. Use a grater to shred the cheese.
3. Roughly chop the garlic.
4. Fill the bread maker with all the ingredients as directed by the manufacturer.
5. Select the appropriate baking setting and start the machine.

Cheesy Pizza Dough

	Ingredients	Nutrition
	• ½ cup warm beer, or more as needed • one tablespoon Parmesan cheese • 1⅓ teaspoon pizza dough yeast • 1 teaspoon salt • 1 teaspoon ground black pepper • 1 teaspoon granulated garlic • one tablespoon olive oil • 5 cups of all-purpose flour, or more if needed	• Calories: 199 • Carbohydrates: 33 g • Cholesterol: 1 mg • Total Fat: 4.3 g • Protein: 5.4 g • Sodium: 330 mg

Directions:

1. In a large bowl, combine granulated garlic, pepper, salt, yeast, Parmesan cheese, and beer. Stir until the salt is dissolved. Let the mixture sit for 4 minutes until the yeast forms a creamy layer. Stir in olive oil.
2. Gradually add flour to the yeast mixture, mixing until the dough is smooth. Adjust consistency with more flour or beer if needed. Allow the dough to rise for an hour. After rising, punch down the dough and roll it out on a floured surface to form a pizza crust.

Collards & Bacon Grilled Pizza

	Ingredients	Nutrition
-	<ul><li>1 lb. whole-wheat pizza dough</li><li>3¼ tablespoons garlic-flavoured olive oil</li><li>2 cups thinly sliced cooked collard greens</li><li>1 cup shredded Cheddar cheese</li><li>¼ cup crumbled cooked bacon</li></ul>	<ul><li>Calories: 491</li><li>Carbohydrates: 50 g</li><li>Cholesterol: 33 mg</li><li>Total Fat: 18 ½ g</li><li>Fiber: 6 g</li><li>Protein: 19 g</li><li>Sodium: 573 mg</li><li>Sugar: 3 g</li></ul>

Directions:

1. Preheat the grill to medium-high heat.
2. On a lightly floured surface, roll the dough into an oval shape about ½ inch thick. Transfer the dough onto a large baking sheet lightly dusted with flour.
3. Brush the grill rack with oil. Carefully place the dough on the grill and cover. Grill for 1-2 minutes, or until the dough is puffy and lightly browned. Use tongs to flip the crust over.
4. Brush the cooked side of the crust with oil. Spread cheddar cheese and collard greens over the grilled side of the crust. Cover the grill again and cook for an additional 2-3 minutes, or until the cheese is melted and the bottom crust is golden brown.

187

Sweet Bread

Brown & White Sugar Bread

	Ingredients	Nutrition
1½-Pound Loaf	• 1 cup milk (room temperature) • ¼ cup butter, softened • 1 egg • ¼ cup light brown sugar • ¼ cup granulated white sugar • 2¼ tablespoons ground cinnamon • ⅓ teaspoon salt • 3 cups bread flour • 2¼ teaspoons bread machine yeast	• Calories: 195 • Total fat: 4 g • Saturated Fat: 2.1½ g • Cholesterol: 25 mg • Sodium: 94 mg • Carbohydrates: 33.3 g • Fiber: 1.6 g • Sugar: 1½ g • Protein: 4.7 g

Directions:

1. Add the ingredients to the bread machine pan following the manufacturer's instructions.
2. Insert the pan into the bread machine and close the lid securely.
3. Choose the Sweet Bread setting and select Medium Crust.
4. Press the Start button to begin the baking process.
5. Once the baking cycle is complete, carefully remove the pan from the bread machine and invert the bread onto a wire rack to cool completely before slicing.
6. Use a sharp knife to slice the bread into desired sizes and serve.

Molasses Bread

	Ingredients	Nutrition
1½-Pound Loaf	• 1/3 cup milk • ¼ cup water • 3¼ tablespoons molasses • 3¼ tablespoons butter, softened • 2 cups bread flour • 1¾ cups whole-wheat flour • 2¼ tablespoons white sugar • 1 teaspoon salt • 2⅓ teaspoons quick-rising yeast	• Calories: 250 • Total Fat: 3.9 g • Saturated Fat: 1.7 g • Cholesterol: 1 mg • Sodium: 230 mg • Carbohydrates: 37.4 g • Fiber: 3.1 g • Sugar: 5.1 g • Protein: 5.6 g •

Directions:

1. Arrange all ingredients in the bread machine pan following the manufacturer's instructions. Insert the pan into the bread machine and close the lid. Set the machine to the light crust option. Press Start. Once the baking cycle is complete, carefully remove the pan from the machine and invert the bread onto a wire rack to cool completely before slicing.
2. Slice the bread into your preferred sizes using a sharp knife and serve.

Honey Bread

	Ingredients	Nutrition
1-Pound Loaf	• 1 cup plus one tablespoon milk • 3¼ tablespoons honey • 3¼ tablespoons butter, melted • 3 cups bread flour • 1⅓ teaspoon salt • 2¼ teaspoons active dry yeast	• Calories: 176 • Total Fat: 2.7 g • Saturated Fat: 1.6 g • Cholesterol: 70 mg • Sodium: 441 mg • Carbohydrates: 22.1 g • Fiber: 0.1½ g • Sugar: 4 g • Protein: 3.3 g

Directions:

1. Add all ingredients to the bread machine's baking pan in the order specified by the manufacturer.

Insert the baking pan into the bread machine and secure the lid.

Choose the White Bread setting and select Medium Crust.

Press the Start button to begin the baking process.

Once the baking cycle is complete, carefully remove the baking pan from the machine and turn the bread onto a wire rack to cool completely before slicing.

Use a sharp knife to cut the bread into desired sizes and serve.

	Ingredients	Nutrition
1½-Pound Loaf	• 1 cup buttermilk • 2¼ tablespoons maple syrup • 2¼ tablespoons vegetable oil • 2¼ tablespoons non-fat dry milk powder • 1 cup whole-wheat flour • 2 cups bread flour • 1 teaspoon salt • 1⅓ teaspoon bread machine yeast	• Calories: 171 • Total Fat: 2.6 g • Saturated Fat: 0.6 g • Cholesterol: 1 mg • Sodium: 230 mg • Total Carbohydrates: 26.1 g • Fiber: 0.4 g • Sugar: 3.1½ g • Protein: 4.7 g

Directions:

1. **Place all the ingredients in the bread machine's baking pan, following the order recommended by the manufacturer.**

2. **Insert the baking pan into the bread machine and close the lid securely.**

3. **Select the Sweet Bread setting on the bread machine.**

4. **Press the Start button to begin the baking process.**

5. **Once the baking cycle is complete, carefully remove the baking pan from the machine and invert the loaf onto a wire rack to cool completely before slicing.**

6. **Using a sharp knife, cut the loaf into the desired-sized pieces and serve.**

Peanut Butter & Jelly Bread

	Ingredients	Nutrition
1½--Pound Loaf	• 1 cup water • 1⅓ tablespoons vegetable oil • ½ cup peanut butter • ½ cup blackberry jelly • one tablespoon white sugar • 1 teaspoon salt • 1 cup whole-wheat flour • 2 cups bread flour • 1⅓ teaspoon active dry yeast	• Calories: 181 • Total Fat: 7.3 g Sat Fat: 1.5 gCholesterol: 0 mg • Sodium: 230 mg • Carbohydrates: 31.6 g • Fiber: 1.1 g • Sugar: 2.7 g • Protein: 6.7 g

Directions:

1. Place all the ingredients in the bread machine's baking pan, following the order recommended by the manufacturer.
2. Insert the baking pan into the bread machine and close the lid securely.
3. Select the Sweet Bread setting on the bread machine.
4. Press the Start button to begin the baking process.
5. Once the baking cycle is complete, carefully remove the baking pan from the machine and invert the loaf onto a wire rack to cool completely before slicing.
6. Use a sharp knife to cut the loaf into the desired-sized pieces and serve.

Raisin Bread

	Ingredients	Nutrition
1½--Pound Loaf	• 1 cup water • 2¼ tablespoons margarine • 3 cups bread flour • 3¼ tablespoons white sugar • 1 teaspoon salt • 1 teaspoon ground cinnamon • 2⅓ teaspoon active dry yeast • ¾ cup golden raisins	• Calories: 182 • Total Fat: 2.3 g • Sat Fat: 0.4 g • Cholesterol: 0 mg • Sodium: 230 mg • Carbohydrates: 34.5 g • Fiber: 1.5 g • Sugar:11 g • Protein: 3.9 g

Directions:

1. Add all ingredients, excluding the raisins, to the bread machine's baking pan following the manufacturer's order.
2. Insert the baking pan into the bread machine and securely close the lid.
3. Select the Sweet Bread setting on the machine.
4. Press the Start button to begin the baking process.
5. When the bread machine beeps to indicate it's time, add the raisins.
6. Once the baking cycle is complete, carefully remove the baking pan from the machine and invert the loaf onto a wire rack to cool completely before slicing.

Currant Bread

	Ingredients	Nutrition
1-Pound Loaf	• 1¼ cups warm milk • 2¼ tablespoons light olive oil • 2¼ tablespoons maple syrup • 3 cups bread flour • 2¼ teaspoons ground cardamom • 1 teaspoon salt • 2¼ teaspoons active dry yeast • ½ cup currants • ½ cup cashews, chopped finely	• Calories: 232 • Total Fat: 7.1 g • Sat Fat: 1.5 g • Cholesterol: 3 mg • Sodium: 155 mg • Carbs: 36.4 g • Fiber: 1.7 g • Sugar: 4.6 g • Protein: 6.4 g

Directions:

1. As directed by the manufacturer, add all ingredients (excluding currants and cashews) to the baking pan of the bread machine.

2. Place the baking pan inside the bread maker and firmly shut the lid.

3. Select the Basic setting on the bread machine and press the Start button to begin the baking process.

4. When the bread maker beeps to indicate it's time, add the cashews and currants.

5. Once the baking cycle is complete, carefully remove the baking pan from the machine and flip the loaf onto a wire rack to cool completely before slicing.

6. Use a sharp knife to slice the bread into the desired sizes and serve.

Pineapple Juice Bread

	Ingredients	Nutrition
1-Pound Loaf	• ¾ cup fresh pineapple juice • 1 egg • 2¼ tablespoons vegetable oil • 2½ tablespoons honey • ¾ teaspoon salt • 3 cups bread flour • 2¼ tablespoons dry milk powder • 2¼ teaspoons quick-rising yeast	• Calories: 181 • Total Fat: 3 g Sat Fat: 0.6 g • Cholesterol: 1 mg • Sodium: 180 mg • Carbohydrates: 30.5 • Fiber: 1 g • Sugar: 6 g • Protein: 4.5 g

Directions:

1. Place all ingredients into the bread machine's baking pan following the manufacturer's instructions.

2. Insert the pan into the bread machine, ensuring it's properly placed, and securely close the lid.

3. Select the Sweet Bread setting on the bread machine and choose the Light Crust option.

4. Press the Start button to begin the baking process.

5. After the baking cycle is complete, carefully remove the pan from the machine and gently invert the loaf onto a wire rack to cool thoroughly before slicing.

6. Use a sharp knife to cut the loaf into your preferred slice sizes and serve.

Buttery Sweet Bread

	Ingredients	Nutrition
1-Pound Loaf	• 1/3 cup water • ½ cup milk • ¼ cup of sugar • 1 beaten egg • 1 teaspoon salt • ¼ cup margarine or ¼ cup butter • 2¼ teaspoons bread machine yeast • 3 1/3 cups bread flour	• Calories: 191 • Carbohydrates: 18½ g • Total fat: 4 g • Protein: 4 g • Fiber: 1 g • Sugars: 3 g • Sodium: 230 mg • Potassium: 50 mg

Directions:

1. Place all the ingredients neatly into the bread machine pan.
2. Select the White Bread setting on your bread machine.
3. Once the baking process is complete, carefully remove the pan and allow it to rest for exactly 11 minutes.

Chocolate Coffee Bread

	Ingredients	Nutrition
	• 1 1/3 cups water • 1/3 cup cocoa powder • 1 1/3 cups bread flour • 1 1/3 cups whole wheat flour • 3 tablespoons powdered milk • 1 1/2 teaspoons salt • 1 1/2 tablespoons honey • 2 1/4 teaspoons active dry yeast • 1/2 cup semi-sweet chocolate chips	• Calories: 179 • Total Fat: 4.6 g • Saturated Fat: 1.1 1/2 g • Cholesterol: 3 mg • Sodium: 230 mg • Carbohydrates: 29 g • Fiber: 1.3 g • Sugars: 5.3 g • Protein: 4.3 g

Directions:

1. Arrange all ingredients in the bread machine pan following the manufacturer's suggested order.
2. Select the Basic Bread cycle on your bread machine and press Start.
3. If your bread machine has a Fruit or Nut dispenser, add the chocolate chips and mocha mix when prompted by the signal, typically about five minutes before the kneading cycle ends.

Cinnamon Sugar Bread

	Ingredients	Nutrition
1-Pound Loaf	• ¼ cup margarine or ¼ cup softened butter • 1 cup milk • 3 cups of bread flour • 1 egg • ½ teaspoon of salt • ½ cup of sugar • 2¼ teaspoons of yeast • 5 teaspoons of cinnamon	• Calories: 180 • Carbohydrates: 18 g • Total fat: 4 g • Cholesterol: 0 mg • Protein: 4 g • Fiber: 1 g • Sugars 3 g • Sodium: 122 mg • Potassium:50 mg

Directions:

1. Place all the ingredients into your bread maker's pan.

2. Select the setting for classic white bread on your bread maker.

3. Once the baking cycle is complete, carefully remove the bread from the pan and let it rest for 5 minutes on a cooling rack before slicing.

Chocolate Bread

	Ingredients	Nutrition
1-Pound Loaf	• 1 pack active dry yeast • ½ cup of sugar • 3 cups bread flour • ¼ cup cocoa powder • 1 large egg • ¼ cup butter • ½ teaspoon vanilla extract • 1 cup milk	• Calories: 184 • Carbohydrates: 31 g • Total fat: 4 g • Cholesterol: 13 mg • Protein: 5 g • Fiber: 3 g • Sugars: 1½ g • Sodium: 18 mgPotassium: 92 mg

Directions:

4. Place all the ingredients into your bread machine's pan.

5. Select the Rapid Bread or equivalent quick setting on your bread machine.

6. Once the baking cycle is complete, remove the pan from the bread machine and let the bread rest for 5 minutes.

Cranberry Walnut Bread

	Ingredients	Nutrition
1-Pound Loaf	• ¼ cup of water • ¼ cup rolled oats • 1 egg • 1 cup buttermilk • 1⅓ tablespoons margarine • 3¼ tablespoons honey • 1 teaspoon salt • 3 cups bread flour • ½ teaspoon ground cinnamon • ⅓ teaspoon baking soda • ¾ cup dried cranberries • 2¼ teaspoons active dry yeast • ½ cup chopped walnuts	• Calories: 180 • Carbohydrates: 31 g • Total fat: 4 g • Cholesterol: 13 mg • Protein: 5 g • Fiber: 3 g • Sugar 1½ g • Sodium: 230 mg • Potassium: 92 mg

Directions:

1. Place all ingredients into the bread machine pan, excluding the walnuts and cranberries.
2. Select the Light Crust and Sweet cycle settings on your bread machine.
3. Press the Start button to begin the baking process.
4. When you hear the beep signal (if your machine has one), add the walnuts and cranberries into the bread machine pan.
5. Once the baking cycle is complete, carefully remove the pan from the machine and let the bread sit for 4-6 minutes.

Coconut Ginger Bread

	Ingredients	Nutrition
1-Pound Loaf	• 1 cup + 2¼ tablespoons Half & Half • 1¼ cups toasted shredded coconut • 2 large eggs • ¼ cup oil • 1 teaspoon coconut extract • 1 teaspoon lemon extract • ¾ cup sugar • one tablespoon grated lemon peel • 2 cups all-purpose flour • 2¼ tablespoons finely chopped candied ginger • 1 teaspoon baking powder • ½ teaspoon salt • 1¼ cups toasted shredded coconut	• Calories: 180Carbohydrates: 40 g • Total Fat: 3 g • Cholesterol: 3 mg • Protein: 5 g • Fiber: 3 g Sugar 15 g • Sodium: 120 mg • Potassium: 61 mg

Directions:

1. Place all ingredients into the bread machine pan.
2. Select the Quick Bread mode on your bread machine.
3. Press the Start button to begin the baking process.
4. Once the bread is baked, allow it to cool on a wire rack for at least 1 minute before serving.

Hawaiian Sweet Bread

	Ingredients	Nutrition
-	• ¾ cup pineapple juice • 1 egg • 2¼ tablespoons vegetable oil • 2 ½ tablespoons honey • ¾ teaspoon salt • 3 cups bread flour 2 • 2¼ tablespoons dry milk • 2¼ teaspoons fast-rising yeast	• Calories: 249 • Carbohydrates: 25 g • Total fat: 4 g • Cholesterol: 25 mg • Protein: 4 g • Fiber: 1 g • Sugars: 5 g • Sodium: 180 mg • Potassium: 76 mg

Directions:

1. Add all the ingredients into the bread machine container.
2. Select the White Bread cycle on your bread machine.
3. Press the Start button to begin the cycle.
4. Once the bread machine has finished baking, remove the pan and let the bread sit for 5 minutes before serving.

Date and Nut Bread

	Ingredients	Nutrition
1-Pound Loaf	• 1⅓ tablespoons vegetable oil • 1 cup of water • ½ teaspoon salt • 2¼ tablespoons honey • ¾ cup whole-wheat flour • ¾ cup rolled oats • 1⅓ teaspoon active dry yeast • 1½ cups bread flour • ½ cup almonds, chopped • ½ cup dates, chopped and pitted	• Calories: 222 • Carbohydrates: 18 g • Fat: 5g • Cholesterol: 0 mg • Protein: 3 g • Fiber: 3 gSugar: 7 g • Sodium: 120 mg • Potassium: 130 mg

Directions:

1. Place all ingredients in the bread machine pan.
2. Select the standard cycle and press start.
3. Remove the pan when finished and let it rest for 5 minutes.

Holiday Bread

Pumpkin Bread

	Ingredients	Nutrition
1 Pound Loaf	<ul><li>½ cup warm water</li><li>½ cup canned pumpkin puree</li><li>¼ cup butter, softened</li><li>¼ cup non-fat dry milk powder</li><li>2 ¾ cups bread flour</li><li>¼ cup brown sugar</li><li>¾ teaspoon salt</li><li>1 teaspoon ground cinnamon</li><li>¾ teaspoon ground ginger</li><li>1½ teaspoons ground nutmeg</li><li>2 teaspoons active dry yeast</li></ul>	<ul><li>Calories: 180</li><li>Total Fat 3.6 g</li><li>Saturated Fat: 2.1 g</li><li>Cholesterol: 9 mg</li><li>Carbohydrates: 22.4 g</li><li>Fiber: 1.1 g</li><li>Sugars: 2.9 g</li><li>Protein: 2.9 g</li></ul>

Directions:

1. Combine all ingredients in the bread machine pan, following the manufacturer's recommended order.
2. Insert the baking pan into the bread machine and ensure the lid is securely closed.
3. Select the Basic setting on the bread machine.
4. Press the start button to initiate the baking process.
5. Once the baking cycle is complete, carefully remove the baking pan from the machine.

6. Invert the bread loaf onto a wire rack to allow it to cool completely before slicing.
7. Use a sharp knife to cut the bread into desired-sized slices.

Pumpkin Cranberry Bread

	Ingredients	Nutrition
1½-Pound Loaf	<ul><li>¾ cup water</li><li>¾ cup canned pumpkin</li><li>3 tablespoons brown sugar</li><li>2 tablespoons vegetable oil</li><li>2 cups all-purpose flour</li><li>1 cup whole-wheat flour</li><li>1 teaspoons salt</li><li>½ cup sweetened dried cranberries</li><li>½ cup walnuts, chopped</li><li>1¾ teaspoons active dry yeast</li></ul>	<ul><li>Calories: 180</li><li>Total Fat: 6 g</li><li>Sat Fat: 0.7 g</li><li>Cholesterol: 0 mg</li><li>Sodium: 320 mg</li><li>Carbs: 31.4 g</li><li>Fiber: 3.2 g</li><li>Sugars: 5.1 g</li><li>Protein: 5.6 g</li></ul>

Directions:

1. Load all the ingredients into the bread machine pan following the manufacturer's instructions.

2. Insert the baking pan into the bread machine and securely close the lid.

3. Select the Basic setting on the bread machine's menu.

4. Start the baking process by pressing the start button.

5. Once the baking cycle is complete, carefully remove the baking pan from the machine.

6. Invert the loaf onto a wire rack to allow it to cool completely before slicing.

7. Use a sharp knife to slice the bread into your preferred-sized portions.

8. Serve and enjoy your delicious homemade bread!

Cranberry Bread Preparation

	Ingredients	Nutrition
Pound Loaf	• 1 cup water • ¼ cup honey • 2 tablespoons butter, softened • 4 cups bread flour • 1 teaspoon salt • 2 teaspoons bread machine yeast • 1 cup dried cranberries	• Calories: 235 • Total Fat: 1.1 g • Saturated Fat: 1 g • Cholesterol: 4 mg • Sodium: 240 mg • Carbohydrates: 21 g • Fiber: 1.2 g • Sugars: 4.6 g • Protein: 3.5 g

Directions:

1. Combine all ingredients, excluding the cranberries, into the bread machine pan following the manufacturer's instructions.

2. Insert the baking pan into the bread machine, ensuring the lid is securely closed.

3. Select the Sweet Bread setting on the machine's menu.

4. Start the baking process by pressing the start button.

5. When you hear the bread machine beep (usually after initial mixing or kneading), gently fold in the cranberries.

6. Once the baking cycle is complete, carefully remove the baking pan from the machine and flip the loaf onto a wire rack to cool completely before slicing.

7. Use a sharp knife to slice the bread into desired-sized pieces and serve.

Cranberry Orange Bread

	Ingredients	Nutrition
Pound Loaf	• 3 cups all-purpose flour • 1 cup dried cranberries • ¾ cup plain yogurt • ½ cup warm water • 3 tablespoons honey • 1¼ tablespoon butter, melted • 2 teaspoons active dry yeast • 1 teaspoons salt • 1 teaspoon orange oil	• Calories: 245 • Total Fat: 2.7 g • Sat Fat: 1 g • Cholesterol: 3 mg • Sodium: 360 mg • Carbohydrates: 30.4 g • Fiber: 1.2 g • Sugars: 5.1 g • Protein: 4 g

Directions:

1. Add all the listed ingredients into the bread machine's baking pan following the manufacturer's recommended order.
2. Place the baking pan inside the bread machine and securely close the lid.
3. Select the Basic setting and choose Light Crust.
4. Start the baking process by pressing the start button.
5. Once the baking cycle is complete, carefully remove the baking pan from the machine. Then, gently invert the loaf onto a wire rack to allow it to cool completely before slicing.

Orange Bread

	Ingredients	Nutrition
1½-Pound Loaf	<ul><li>1 cups water</li><li>3 tablespoons powdered milk</li><li>1½ tablespoons vegetable oil</li><li>3 tablespoons honey</li><li>2½ cups bread flour</li><li>¾ cup amaranth flour</li><li>1/3 cup whole-wheat flour</li><li>½ teaspoon salt</li><li>3 tablespoons fresh orange zest, grated finely</li><li>2 teaspoons active dry yeast</li></ul>	<ul><li>Calories: 205</li><li>Total Fat: 2.9 g</li><li>Sat Fat: 0.6 g</li><li>Cholesterol: 0 mg</li><li>Sodium: 182 mg</li><li>Carbohydrates: 36.9 g</li><li>Fiber: 2.2 g</li><li>Sugars: 5.6 g</li><li>Protein: 6 g</li></ul>

Directions:

1. Arrange all ingredients in the bread machine's baking pan according to the manufacturer's instructions.

2. Insert the baking pan into the bread machine and securely close the lid.

3. Select the Basic setting from the menu options.

4. Start the baking process by pressing the start button.

5. Once the baking cycle is complete, carefully remove the baking pan from the machine. Invert the loaf onto a wire rack to cool completely before slicing.

Banana Chocolate Chip Bread

	Ingredients	Nutrition
Pound Loaf	<ul><li>½ cup warm milk</li><li>2 eggs</li><li>½ cup butter, melted</li><li>1½ teaspoon vanilla extract</li><li>3 medium ripe bananas, peeled and mashed</li><li>1 cup granulated white sugar</li><li>2 cups all-purpose flour</li><li>½ teaspoon salt</li><li>2 teaspoons baking powder</li><li>1 teaspoon baking soda</li><li>½ cup chocolate chips</li></ul>	<ul><li>Calories: 215</li><li>Total Fat: 1½ g</li><li>Saturated Fat: 5 g</li><li>Cholesterol: 31½ mg</li><li>Sodium: 125 mg</li><li>Carbohydrates: 33.4 g</li><li>Fiber: 1.2 g</li><li>Sugars: 11 g</li><li>Protein: 3 g</li></ul>

Directions:

1. Combine all ingredients, excluding the cranberries, in the bread machine's baking pan following the manufacturer's instructions.
2. Insert the baking pan into the bread machine and securely close the lid.
3. Choose the Quick Bread setting on the bread machine's menu.
4. Start the baking process by pressing the start button.
5. When you hear the beep signal from the bread machine (usually after initial mixing or kneading), add the chocolate chips to the mixture.
6. After the baking cycle completes, carefully remove the baking pan from the machine. Invert the loaf onto a wire rack to allow it to cool completely before slicing.

Sweet Potato Bread

	Ingredients	Nutrition
Pound Loaf	<ul><li>½ cup warm water</li><li>1 teaspoon pure vanilla extract</li><li>1 cup boiled sweet potato, peeled, and mashed</li><li>4 cups bread flour</li><li>½ teaspoon ground cinnamon</li><li>2 tablespoons butter, softened</li><li>1/3 cup brown sugar</li><li>1 teaspoon salt</li><li>2 teaspoons active dry yeast</li><li>2 tablespoons powdered milk</li></ul>	<ul><li>Calories: 195</li><li>Total Fat: 1.1 g</li><li>Sat Fat: 1 g</li><li>Cholesterol: 4 mg</li><li>Protein: 4 g</li><li>Sodium: 249 mg</li><li>Carbs: 30.2 g</li><li>Fiber: 1.2 g</li><li>Sugars: 4.4 g</li></ul>

Directions:

1. Combine all ingredients in the bread machine's baking pan, following the manufacturer's suggested order.
2. Insert the baking pan into the bread machine and securely close the lid.
3. Select the White Bread setting from the bread machine's menu options.
4. Start the baking process by pressing the start button.
5. Once the baking cycle is complete, carefully remove the baking pan from the machine and invert the bread loaf onto a wire rack to cool completely before slicing.

Gingerbread

	Ingredients	Nutrition
1½ Pounds Loaf	<ul><li>¾ cup milk</li><li>¼ cup molasses</li><li>1 egg</li><li>3 tablespoons butter</li><li>3 cups bread flour</li><li>1½ tablespoon brown sugar</li><li>¾ teaspoon salt</li><li>¾ teaspoon ground cinnamon</li><li>¾ teaspoon ground ginger</li><li>2¼ teaspoons active dry yeast</li><li>1/3 cup raisins</li></ul>	<ul><li>Calories: 210</li><li>Total Fat: 4 g</li><li>Saturated Fat: 2.2 g</li><li>Cholesterol: 23 mg</li><li>Sodium: 180 mg</li><li>Carbohydrates: 36 g</li><li>Fiber: 1.3 g</li><li>Sugars: 7.5 g</li><li>Protein: 5 g</li></ul>

Directions:

1. Add all the listed ingredients, excluding raisins, into the bread machine's baking pan, following the manufacturer's recommended order.
2. Place the baking pan securely into the bread machine and close the lid.
3. Select the Basic setting and adjust the crust setting to Light.
4. Start the baking process by pressing the start button.
5. When you hear the beep from the bread machine indicating it's time to add ingredients (usually after initial mixing or kneading), add the raisins.
6. After baking, carefully remove the baking pan from the machine and invert the bread onto a wire rack to cool completely before slicing.

.

Raisin Cinnamon Swirl Bread

	Ingredients	Nutrition
1½-Pound Loaf	**Dough** • ¼ cup milk • 1 egg, beaten • Water, as required • ¼ cup butter, softened • 1/3 cup white sugar • 1 teaspoon salt • 3½ cups bread flour • 2 teaspoons active dry yeast • ½ cup raisins **Cinnamon Swirl** • 1/3 cup white sugar • 3 teaspoons ground cinnamon • 2 egg whites, beaten • 1/3 cup butter, melted and cooled	• Calories: 290 • Total Fat: 11 g • Sat Fat: 6.5 g • Cholesterol: 41 mg • Sodium: 277 mg • Carbs: 6.2 g • Fiber: 1.5 g • Sugars: 11 g • Protein: 5.5 g

Directions:

1. In a small bowl, combine milk and egg.
2. Adjust with water to make a total of 1 cup of liquid mixture.
3. Pour the egg mixture into the bread machine's baking pan.
4. Add the remaining ingredients (excluding raisins) on top according to the manufacturer's instructions.
5. Insert the baking pan into the bread machine and close the lid.
6. Select the Dough cycle on the bread machine.
7. Press the start button to begin the process.
8. When prompted by the bread machine (usually after initial mixing or kneading), add the raisins.
9. Once the Dough cycle completes, remove the dough from the bread pan and place it on a lightly floured surface.
10. Shape the dough into a rectangle measuring 1¼ inches thick and 1½ inches wide.

For the swirl:
1. Combine the sugar and cinnamon in a mixing bowl.
2. Brush the dough rectangle with 1 egg white followed by melted butter.
3. Sprinkle the cinnamon sugar mixture evenly over the dough, leaving a 1-inch border on all sides.
4. Starting from one of the shorter ends, roll the dough tightly into a log and pinch the ends to seal.
5. Grease a loaf pan and place the rolled dough into it.
6. Cover the loaf pan with a kitchen towel and let it rest in a warm spot for 1 hour or until doubled in size.
7. Preheat your oven to 350°F (175°C).
8. Brush the surface of the dough with the remaining egg white.
9. Bake for approximately 35 minutes or until a wooden skewer inserted into the center comes out clean.
10. Once baked, remove the bread from the oven and let it cool in the loaf pan on a wire rack for about 15 minutes.
11. Allow the bread to cool completely before slicing.

Chocolate Chip Bread

	Ingredients	Nutrition
1½-Pound Loaf	<ul><li>1 cup milk</li><li>¼ cup water</li><li>1 egg, beaten</li><li>2 tablespoons butter, softened</li><li>3 cups bread flour</li><li>2¼ tablespoons white sugar</li><li>1 teaspoon salt</li><li>1 teaspoon ground cinnamon</li><li>1½ teaspoons active dry yeast</li><li>¾ cup semi-sweet mini chocolate chips</li></ul>	<ul><li>Calories: 230</li><li>Total Fat: 7 g</li><li>Sat Fat: 4.1 g</li><li>Cholesterol: 1 mg</li><li>Sodium: 240 mg</li><li>Carbohydrates: 36.2 g</li><li>Fiber: 1.1 g</li><li>Sugars: 5.1 g</li><li>Protein: 4.7 g</li></ul>

Directions: for the dough:

1. Combine all ingredients (excluding the chocolate chips) in the baking pan of the bread machine, following the manufacturer's recommended order.

2. Insert the baking pan into the bread machine and securely close the lid.

3. Choose the "Mix Bread" or "Basic" setting on the bread machine.

4. Press the start button to initiate the mixing process.

5. When prompted by the bread machine (usually after the initial mixing or kneading cycle), add the chocolate chips.

6. Once the mixing cycle is complete, carefully remove the baking pan from the machine.

7. Invert the bread onto a wire rack and allow it to cool completely before slicing

Zucchini bread

	Ingredients	Nutrition
2-Pound Loaf	<ul><li>Dark brown sugar 2 tablespoons</li><li>Whole wheat flour 1 ⅓ cups</li><li>Fast-rising yeast or Bread machine yeast 2 ¼ teaspoons (or 2 ¾ teaspoons for bread machine)</li><li>Gluten 1 tablespoon + 1 teaspoon</li><li>Shredded zucchini 1 ½ cups</li><li>Olive oil 3 tablespoons</li><li>Lemon zest Zest of 1 lemon</li><li>Salt 2 teaspoons</li><li>Nonfat milk 1 cup</li><li>Bread flour 2 ⅔ cups</li></ul>	<ul><li>Calories: 180</li><li>Carbohydrates: 14 g</li><li>Cholesterol: 5 mg</li><li>Total Fat: 2.3 g</li><li>Protein: 1.3 g</li></ul>

Directions:

1. Place all the ingredients in the bread machine pan, following the order specified in the manufacturer's instructions.

2. Set the crust option to medium, program the Basic cycle; then press Start.

3. Once the baking cycle is complete, remove the bread from the pan and transfer it to a cooling rack.

4. Allow the bread to cool to room temperature before slicing for optimal texture and flavor.

5. Consider adding a personal touch by experimenting with additional ingredients like nuts, seeds, or dried fruits in future batches.

Multi-Grain Bread

French Crusty Loaf Bread

	Ingredients	Nutrition
2-Pound Loaf	• 5 slices bread • 2 cups + 2¼ tablespoons water, lukewarm • 4 teaspoons sugar • 2¼ teaspoons table salt • 6½ cups white bread flour • 2¼ teaspoons bread machine yeast • 1½ slices bread (1 ½ pound) • 1½ cups + one tablespoon water, lukewarm between 1 1/1 and 90° F • 3 teaspoons sugar • 1⅓ teaspoon table salt • 4¾ cups white bread flour • 1⅓ teaspoon bread machine yeast •	• Calories: 176 • Fat 1.3 g • Carbohydrates: 31.4 g • Sodium: 426 mg • Protein: 5.7 g

Directions:
1. Select the desired loaf size and measure your ingredients accordingly.
2. Add the ingredients to the bread pan in the order listed above.
3. Insert the bread pan into the bread machine and close the lid securely.
4. Turn on the bread maker. Choose the French setting, select the pound size, and set the crust color preference. Then, start the cycle.
5. Once the baking cycle is complete and the bread is baked, carefully remove the pan from the machine using a potholder. Allow the bread to rest for a few minutes before slicing and serving.

Oat Molasses Bread

	Ingredients	Nutrition
2-Pound Loaf	• 5 slices bread (2 pounds) • 1 1/3 cups boiling water • ¾ cup old-fashioned oats • 3¼ tablespoons butter • 1 large egg, lightly beaten • 2¼ teaspoons salt • ¼ cup honey • 1⅓ tablespoons dark molasses • 4 cups white bread flour • 2⅓ teaspoon bread machine yeast • 1 ½ slice bread (1½ pounds) • 1 cup boiling water • ½ cup old-fashioned oats • 2¼ tablespoons butter • 1 large egg, lightly beaten • 1⅓ teaspoon table salt • 3¼ tablespoons honey • one tablespoon dark molasses • 3 cups white bread flour • 2¼ teaspoons bread machine yeast	• Calories: 187 • Fat: 7.1 g • Carbohydrates: 11 g • Sodium: 404 mg • Protein: 5.1 g

Directions:

1. In a mixing bowl, combine the oats and boiling water. Allow the oats to soak completely and cool without draining the water.
2. Measure out the ingredients according to the desired bread size.
3. Pour the soaked oats into the bread pan, including any leftover water.
4. Add the remaining ingredients to the bread pan in the specified order.
5. Place the bread pan inside the bread maker and close the lid securely.
6. Turn on the bread maker. Select the Basic setting, choose the desired crust color and loaf size, then start the cycle.
7. Using a potholder, remove the bread pan once the baking cycle is complete. Allow the bread to rest for a few minutes.
8. Remove the bread from the pan and place it on a wire cooling rack. Let it cool for at least a minute before slicing and serving.

English muffin Bread

	Ingredients	Nutrition
1-Pound Loaf	• 1 teaspoon vinegar • ¼ to 1/3 cup water • 1 cup lukewarm milk • 2¼ tablespoons butter or 2¼ tablespoons vegetable oil • 1⅓ teaspoon salt • 1⅓ teaspoon sugar • ½ teaspoon baking powder • 3½ cups unbleached all-purpose flour • 2⅓ teaspoons instant yeast	• Calories: 262 • Carbohydrates: 13 g • Fat: 1 g • Protein: 3 g • Sodium: 360 mg

Directions:

1. Layer each ingredient into the bread maker according to the order and temperature specified in your bread machine's manual.

2. Close the lid, select the Basic bread setting with a light crust, and press Start.

3. Once the baking cycle is complete, remove the bread from the bread maker and transfer it to a cooling rack.

Whole Wheat Corn Bread

	Ingredients	Nutrition
1-Poun d Loaf	• 5 slices bread (2 pounds) • 1 1/3 cups lukewarm water • 2¼ tablespoons light brown sugar • 1 large egg, beaten • 2¼ tablespoons unsalted butter, melted • 1⅓ teaspoon table salt • ¾ cup whole wheat flour • ¾ cup cornmeal • 2¾ cups white bread flour • 2⅓ teaspoon bread machine yeast • 1½ slices bread (1½ pounds) • 1 cup lukewarm water • 1⅓ tablespoons light brown sugar • 1 medium egg, beaten • 1⅓ tablespoons unsalted butter, melted • 1⅓ teaspoon table salt • ½ cup whole wheat flour • ½ cup cornmeal • 2 cups of white bread flour • 1⅓ teaspoon bread machine yeast	• Calories: 194 • Fat: 5.7 g • Carbohydrates: 19.3 g • Sodium: 474 mg • Protein: 4.1 g

Directions:

1. Select the desired loaf size and gather your ingredients.
2. Place the ingredients into the bread pan in the order listed above.
3. Insert the bread pan into the bread machine and close the lid securely.
4. Turn on the bread maker. Choose the Basic setting, select the loaf size, and choose the crust color preference. Then, start the cycle.
5. Once the baking cycle is complete and the bread is baked, use a potholder to carefully remove the bread pan from the machine. Allow it to rest for a few minutes.
6. Remove the bread from the pan and place it on a wire cooling rack. Let it cool for at least 1 minute before slicing and serving.

Wheat Bran Bread e

	Ingredients	Nutrition
1-Pound Loaf	• 5 slices bread (2 pounds) • 1½ cups lukewarm milk • 3¼ tablespoons unsalted butter, melted • ¼ cup of sugar • 2¼ teaspoons table salt • ½ cup wheat bran • 3½ cups white bread flour • 2¼ teaspoons bread machine yeast • 1½ slices bread (1½ pounds) • 1½ cups lukewarm milk • 2¼ tablespoons unsalted butter, melted • 3¼ tablespoons sugar • 1⅓ teaspoon table salt • 1/3 cup wheat bran • 2 2/3 cups of white bread flour • 1⅓ teaspoon bread machine yeast	• Calories: 184 • Fat: 2.1 g • Carbohydrates: 24.6 g • Sodium: 332 mg

Directions:

1. Determine the desired loaf size and adjust the ingredient measurements accordingly.
2. Place the ingredients into the bread machine pan in the specified sequence.
3. Insert the bread pan into the bread maker and close the lid securely.
4. Start the bread machine. Select the loaf size, choose the Basic setting, and set the crust color preference. Then, start the cycle.
5. Use a potholder to carefully remove the bread pan from the machine when the baking cycle is complete. Allow the bread to rest for a few minutes.
6. Carefully remove the bread from the pan and transfer it to a wire cooling rack. Let it cool for at least one minute before slicing and serving.

White Breads

Extra Buttery White Bread

	Ingredients	Nutrition
1½-Pound Loaf	<ul><li>1½ cups milk</li><li>4 tablespoons unsalted butter</li><li>3 cups bread flour</li><li>1½ tablespoons white granulated sugar</li><li>2 teaspoons salt</li><li>1½ teaspoons bread machine yeast</li></ul>	<ul><li>Calories: 180</li><li>Sodium: 360 mg</li><li>Carbohydrates: 20 g</li><li>Fat: 1 g</li><li>Protein: 4 g</li></ul>

Directions:

1. Melt the butter slightly in the microwave until softened.
2. Add all the ingredients to the bread machine, following the order and temperature guidelines provided by the manufacturer.
3. Close the lid, select the basic or white bread setting with a medium crust, and press start.
4. Once the baking cycle is complete, remove the bread and place it on a cooling rack.

Mom's White Brea

	Ingredients	Nutrition
1½-Pound Loaf	<ul><li>1 cup water</li><li>2 tablespoons vegetable oil</li><li>1 teaspoons salt</li><li>2½ tablespoons sugar</li><li>3 cups white bread flour</li><li>2 teaspoons active dry yeast</li></ul>	<ul><li>Calories: 170</li><li>Carbohydrates: 11 g</li><li>Fat: 3 g</li><li>Protein: 90 g</li><li>Sodium: 365 mg</li></ul>

Directions:

1. Place each ingredient into the bread machine following the order and temperature guidelines provided by the manufacturer.

2. Close the lid, select the basic or white bread setting with a medium crust, and press start.

3. Once the baking cycle is complete, remove the bread and place it on a cooling rack.

Vegan White Bread

	Ingredients	Nutrition
2 Pound Loaf	<ul><li>1 ½ cups water</li><li>1/3 cup plant milk (if you can - use silk soy original)</li><li>1 teaspoons salt</li><li>2½ tablespoons white sugar</li><li>2 tablespoons vegetable oil</li><li>3½ cups all-purpose flour</li><li>1¾ teaspoons bread machine yeast</li></ul>	<ul><li>Calories: 170</li><li>Carbohydrates: 13 g</li><li>Fat: 2 g</li><li>Protein: 3.2 g</li><li>Sodium: 360 mg</li></ul>

Directions:

1. Place the ingredients into the bread machine in the order and at the temperature specified by the manufacturer.
2. Close the lid, select the basic or white bread setting with a medium crust, and start the machine.
3. Once baking is complete, remove the bread from the machine and let it cool on a rack.

Rice Flour Rice Bread

	Ingredients	Nutrition
2 Pound Loaf	<ul><li>3 eggs</li><li>1½ cups water</li><li>3 tablespoons vegetable oil</li><li>1 teaspoon apple cider vinegar</li><li>2¼ teaspoons active dry yeast</li><li>3 cups white rice flour</li><li>2½ teaspoons Xanthan gum</li><li>1½ teaspoons salt</li><li>½ cup dry milk powder</li><li>3 tablespoons white sugar</li></ul>	<ul><li>Calories: 195</li><li>Carbohydrates: 24 g</li><li>Fat: 1.2 g</li><li>Protein: 2.2 g</li><li>Sodium: 360 mg</li></ul>

Directions:

4. In a medium bowl, combine the oil, water, eggs, and vinegar.

5. In a separate large bowl, whisk together the yeast, salt, xanthan gum, dry milk powder, rice flour, and sugar.

6. Add the ingredients to the bread machine following the order and temperature specified by the manufacturer.

7. Close the lid, select the whole wheat setting with a medium crust, and start the bread machine.

8. Once baking is complete, remove the bread from the machine and place it on a cooling rack.

Italian White Bread

	Ingredients	Nutrition
Pound Loaf	<ul><li>¾ cup cold water</li><li>2 cups bread flour</li><li>1¼ tablespoon sugar</li><li>1 teaspoon salt</li><li>1¼ tablespoon olive oil</li><li>1 teaspoon active dry yeast</li></ul>	<ul><li>Calories: 171</li><li>Carbohydrates: 11 g</li><li>Fat: 1.1 g</li><li>Protein: 2.2 g</li><li>Sodium: 240 mg</li></ul>

Directions:

1. Place each ingredient into the bread machine in the sequence and at the temperature advised by the manufacturer.

2. Close the lid, select the Italian or basic bread setting with a light crust option, and press start.

3. When the baking cycle is complete, remove the bread from the machine and place it on a cooling rack.

Anadama White Bread

	Ingredients	Nutrition
1½-Pound Loaf	<ul><li>1½ cups warm water</li><li>1/3 cup molasses</li><li>1½ tablespoons butter at room temperature</li><li>1 teaspoon salt</li><li>1/3 cup yellow cornmeal</li><li>3 cups bread flour</li><li>2½ teaspoons bread machine yeast</li></ul>	<ul><li>Calories: 186</li><li>Carbohydrates: 19 g</li><li>Fat: 0.9 g</li><li>Protein: 2 g</li><li>Sodium: 235 mg</li></ul>

Directions:

1. Place each ingredient into the bread maker according to the manufacturer's instructions for order and temperature.
2. Secure the lid, select the basic bread option with a light crust setting, and start the bread machine.
3. Once the baking cycle is complete, remove the bread from the machine and transfer it to a cooling rack.

Soft White Bread

	Ingredients	Nutrition
2 Pound Loaf	<ul><li>2 cups water</li><li>3 teaspoons yeast</li><li>6 tablespoons sugar</li><li>½ cup vegetable oil</li><li>2 teaspoons salt</li><li>3 cups white flour</li></ul>	<ul><li>Calories: 204</li><li>Carbohydrates: 11 g</li><li>Fat: 1 g</li><li>Protein: 4 g</li><li>Sodium: 475 mg</li></ul>

Directions:

1. Place all the ingredients into the bread machine following the recommended order and temperature specified by the manufacturer.
2. Close the lid, choose the basic bread setting, and select the light crust option on your bread machine. Then, start the baking process.
3. Once the bread machine finishes baking, remove the bread and transfer it to a cooling rack.

Dough Recipes

Swedish Cardamom

	Ingredients	Nutrition
Pound Loaf	<ul><li>¼ cup of sugar</li><li>¾ cup of warm milk</li><li>¾ teaspoon cardamom</li><li>½ teaspoon salt</li><li>¼ cup of softened butter</li><li>1 egg</li><li>2¼ teaspoons bread machine yeast</li><li>3 cups all-purpose flour</li><li>5 tablespoons milk for brushing</li><li>2 tablespoons sugar for sprinkling</li></ul>	<ul><li>Calories: 185</li><li>Carbohydrates: 22 g</li><li>Total Fat: 7 g</li><li>Cholesterol: 1 mg</li><li>Protein: 3 g</li><li>Fiber: 1 g</li><li>Sugars: 3 g</li><li>Sodium: 145 mg</li></ul>

Directions:

1. Add all ingredients except milk and sugar into the bread machine pan.
2. Choose the dough cycle and press start. Ensure the dough doubles in size and is elastic and smooth.
3. Transfer the dough to a floured surface.
4. Divide the dough into three balls and let them rest for 5 minutes.

5. Roll each ball into a 1-inch thick rope.

6. Braid the ropes together, tucking the ends underneath, and place on a cookie sheet.

7. Brush with milk and lightly sprinkle with sugar.

8. Bake at 375°F for 25 minutes, covering with foil for the last 5 minutes to prevent over-browning.

9. Cool on a rack.

Pita Bread

	Ingredients	Nutrition
1½-PoundLoaf	• 3 cups of all-purpose flour • 1½ cups warm water • 1¼ tablespoon of vegetable oil • 1 teaspoon salt • 1½ teaspoons active dry yeast • 1 active teaspoon white sugar	• Calories: 190 • Carbohydrates: 37 g • Total Fat: 3 g • Cholesterol: 0 mg • Protein: 5 g • Fiber: 1 g • Sugars: 1 g • Sodium: 243 mg • Potassium: 66 mg

Directions:

1. Add all ingredients to the bread pan.

2. Set the machine to the dough setting and press start.

3. Once the machine signals completion, turn the dough out onto a floured surface.

4. Roll the dough into a 1½-inch rope, then cut it into eight pieces.

5. Shape each piece into a ball, then flatten into a 7-inch circle. Cover with a towel on a floured surface and let rest for 30 minutes until slightly puffy.

6. Preheat your oven to 500°F (260°C).

7. Place the pitas on a wire cake rack and then directly on the oven rack.

8. Bake for 5 minutes or until puffed and lightly browned.

9. Remove from the oven and immediately place the pitas in a sealed paper bag or cover with a damp towel.

10. Split or cut as desired when they are soft.

Butter Bread Rolls

	Ingredients	Nutrition
24 Rolls	-	• 1 cup warm milk • ½ cup butter or ½ cup margarine, softened • ¼ cup sugar • 2 eggs • 1 teaspoons salt • 4 cups bread flour • 2¼ teaspoons active dry yeast	• Calories: 211 • Carbohydrates: 31 g • Fat: 2 g • Protein: 4.1 g • Sodium: 360 mg

Directions:

1. Begin by adding all the ingredients into the bread machine pan, following the sequence recommended by the machine's manufacturer.

2. Choose the dough setting on your machine.

3. Once the cycle finishes, transfer the dough to a lightly floured surface.

4. Cut the dough into 24 equal portions.

5. Form each portion into a neat ball.

6. Arrange the balls in a greased 13x9-inch baking pan.

7. Cover the pan and allow the dough to rise in a warm spot for 30-45 minutes.

8. Bake at 350°F for 14-16 minutes, or until the tops are golden brown.

Lemon and Poppy Buns

	Ingredients	Nutrition
1½-Pound loaf	<ul><li>Melted Butter for grease</li><li>1 1/3 cups hot water</li><li>3¼ tablespoons powdered milk</li><li>2¼ tablespoons Crisco shortening</li><li>1½ teaspoon salt</li><li>one tablespoon lemon juice</li><li>4¼ cups bread flour</li><li>½ teaspoon nutmeg</li><li>2¼ teaspoons grated lemon rind</li><li>2¼ tablespoons poppy seeds</li><li>1⅓ teaspoons yeast</li><li>2¼ teaspoons wheat gluten</li></ul>	<ul><li>Calories: 231</li><li>Carbohydrates: 31 g</li><li>Total Fat: 11 g</li><li>Sugar: 1½ g</li><li>Fiber: 1 g</li><li>Sodium: 230 mg</li><li>Protein: 4 g</li></ul>

Directions:

1. Fill your bread machine with all the ingredients, excluding the melted butter.

2. Select the "Dough" cycle on the bread machine and let it run.

3. When the cycle is finished, remove the dough and place it on a floured board.

4. Let the dough rest for five minutes, covered lightly with plastic wrap or a kitchen towel.

5. Divide the dough into fifteen equal pieces and shape each piece into a ball.

6. Grease a large cookie sheet with butter.

7. Place the dough balls on the sheet, ensuring space between them to allow for expansion.

8. Cover the dough balls and let them rise in a warm place until doubled in size, about 30 to 40 minutes.

9. Preheat the oven to 375°F. Bake the rolls for 15 to 20 minutes until they are golden brown.

Multigrain Sourdough Bread

	Ingredients	Nutrition
1-Pound Loaf	<ul><li>2 cups sourdough starter</li><li>2¼ tablespoons butter or</li><li>2¼ tablespoons olive oil</li><li>½ cup milk</li><li>1 cup water</li><li>1 teaspoon salt</li><li>¼ cup honey</li><li>½ cup sunflower seeds</li><li>½ cup millet or ½ cup amaranth or ½ cup quinoa</li><li>3½ cups multi-grain flour</li></ul>	<ul><li>Calories: 180</li><li>Carbs: 13.5 g</li><li>Total Fat: 1.1 g</li><li>Protein: 2.7 g</li><li>Fiber: 1.4 g</li><li>Sodium: 230 mg</li></ul>

Directions:

1. Add all ingredients to the bread machine pan.
2. Select the dough cycle on the bread machine.
3. Conventional Oven:
4. Once the cycle completes, remove the dough and place it on a lightly floured surface, shaping it into a loaf.
5. Place the shaped dough in a greased loaf pan, cover, and let it rise until it is a couple of inches above the pan's edge.
6. Bake at 370°F for 50 minutes.

Sourdough Boule

	Ingredients	Nutrition
1½-Pound Loaf	<ul><li>1 cup water</li><li>500 g sourdough starter</li><li>550 g all-purpose flour</li><li>1 g salt</li></ul>	<ul><li>Calories: 230</li><li>Fat: 0.7 g</li><li>Protein: 6.9 g</li><li>Sodium: 10 mg</li></ul>

Directions:

1. Begin by combining the flour, warm water, and starter, and allow it to rest, covered, for at least 30 minutes.
2. After the resting period, mix in the salt and transfer the dough onto a floured surface.
3. Gently flatten the dough and fold it in half a few times.
4. Cover the dough and let it rise for 2-4 hours, performing the slap and fold technique a few more times during this period.
5. Once the dough doubles in size, gently stretch it to tighten the top surface. Let it rise for another 2-4 hours.
6. Preheat the oven to 475° F and place a baking stone or cast iron pan inside to preheat.
7. Transfer the risen dough onto the preheated stone or pan, score the top, and bake for 1 minute at 475° F, then reduce the heat to 425° F and bake for 25-35 minutes until golden brown.

Herbed Baguette

	Ingredients	Nutrition
1½-Pound Loaf	<ul><li>5 cups warm water</li><li>2 cups sourdough starter, either fed or unfed</li><li>4 to 5 cups all-purpose flour</li><li>2⅓ teaspoon salt</li><li>2¼ teaspoons sugar</li><li>one tablespoon instant yeast</li><li>one tablespoon fresh oregano, chopped</li><li>1 teaspoon fresh rosemary, chopped</li><li>one tablespoon fresh basil, chopped</li><li>Any other desired herbs</li></ul>	<ul><li>Calories: 197</li><li>Fat: 0.6 g</li><li>Protein: 5.1 g</li><li>Carbs: 10 g</li><li>Sodium: 400 mg</li></ul>

Directions:

1. Combine all ingredients in the bowl of a mixer. Use a dough hook to knead the mixture until a smooth dough forms, about 4-6 minutes. Add more flour if needed to achieve the right consistency.

2. Oil a bowl, place the dough inside, cover it, and let it rest for approximately 2 hours.

3. After the dough has rested, divide it into three equal parts. Shape each portion into a loaf about 5 inches long, using a rolling and folding technique.

4. Arrange the shaped baguettes on lined baking sheets, cover them, and let them rise for one hour.

5. Preheat the oven to 425°F and bake the baguettes for 25 minutes until they are golden brown.

French Sourdough Bread

	Ingredients	Nutrition
1-Pound Loaf	<ul><li>2 cups sourdough starter</li><li>1 teaspoon salt</li><li>½ cup water</li><li>4 cups white bread flour</li><li>2¼ tablespoons white cornmeal</li></ul>	<ul><li>Calories: 167</li><li>Carbohydrates: 196 g</li><li>Total Fat: 0.4 g</li><li>Protein: 26.5 g</li><li>Sodium: 230 mg</li><li>Fiber: 7.3 g</li></ul>

Directions:

1. Place all ingredients into the bread machine pan, keeping the cornmeal aside.

2. Select the dough cycle on the bread machine.

3. Preheat the oven to 375°F.

4. When the dough cycle finishes, transfer the dough to a floured surface.

5. Add extra flour if the dough is too sticky.

6. Divide the dough into two parts and shape each into an oval about 1½ inches thick.

7. Fold the ovals in half lengthwise and pinch the seams to form elongated shapes.

8. Sprinkle cornmeal on a baking sheet and place the loaves seam-side down.

9. Cover and let rise until doubled in size.

10. Place a deep pan filled with hot water on the oven's bottom shelf.

11. Make shallow, diagonal slashes on the tops of the loaves with a knife.

12. Place the loaves in the oven and mist them with water using a spray bottle. Spray the oven walls as well.

13. Repeat the misting process three times at one-minute intervals.

14. Remove the pan of water after 15 minutes of baking.

15. Continue baking for 30 to 40 minutes or until the loaves are golden brown.

Garlic and Herb Flatbread Sourdough

	Ingredients	Nutrition
1½-Poun d Loaf	<ul><li>Dough</li><li>1 cup sourdough starter, fed or unfed</li><li>¾ cup warm water</li><li>2¼ teaspoons instant yeast</li><li>3 cups all-purpose flour</li><li>1⅓ teaspoon salt</li><li>3¼ tablespoons olive oil</li><li>Topping</li><li>½ teaspoon dried thyme</li><li>½ teaspoon dried oregano</li><li>½ teaspoon dried marjoram</li><li>1 teaspoon garlic powder</li><li>⅓ teaspoon onion powder</li><li>⅓ teaspoon salt</li><li>⅓ teaspoon pepper</li><li>3¼ tablespoons olive oil</li></ul>	<ul><li>Calories: 129</li><li>Fat: 3.7 g</li><li>Protein: 1.1 g</li><li>Sodium: 120 mg</li><li>Carbohydrate s: 10 g</li></ul>

Directions:

1. Combine all the dough ingredients in a stand mixer bowl and knead until smooth. Allow the dough to rise in a lightly greased bowl for at least one hour. After punching down the dough, let it rise again for another hour.

2. For the topping, mix all ingredients except the olive oil in a small bowl.

3. Lightly grease a 9x13 baking pan or standard baking sheet. Pat and roll the dough into a long rectangle in the pan. Brush olive oil over the dough and sprinkle the herb and seasoning mixture on top. Cover and let it rise for 5-10 minutes.

4. Preheat the oven to 425°F and bake for 25-30 minutes until golden brown.

Dinner Rolls

Ingredients	Nutrition
<ul><li>1 cup sourdough starter</li><li>1½ cups warm water</li><li>one tablespoon yeast</li><li>one tablespoon salt</li><li>2¼ tablespoons sugar</li><li>2¼ tablespoons olive oil</li><li>5 cups all-purpose flour</li><li>2¼ tablespoons butter, melted</li></ul>	<ul><li>Calories: 191</li><li>Fat: 2.2 g</li><li>Protein: 3.3 g</li><li>Carbohydrates: 13 g</li><li>Sodium: 230 mg</li><li>Sugar: 1.1 g</li></ul>

Directions:

1. Begin by combining sourdough starter, water, yeast, salt, sugar, and oil in a large bowl. Stir in flour until a dough forms, adding more flour if necessary. Transfer the dough to a greased bowl and let it rise until doubled in size, approximately 2 hours.

2. After the dough has risen, divide it into pieces approximately 2-3 inches in size. Place the buns in a greased 9x13 pan, cover, and allow them to rise for about an hour.

3. Preheat the oven to 350° F. Bake the rolls for 15 minutes, then remove them from the oven. Brush the tops with melted butter and return to the oven for an additional 5-10 minutes.

Olive and Garlic Sourdough Bread

	Ingredients	Nutrition
1-Pound Loaf	<ul><li>2 cups sourdough starter</li><li>1 cup water</li><li>3 cups flour</li><li>2¼ tablespoons olive oil</li><li>2¼ tablespoons sugar</li><li>2¼ teaspoons salt</li><li>½ cup chopped black olives</li><li>6 cloves chopped garlic</li></ul>	<ul><li>Calories: 180</li><li>Carbohydrate: 26.5 g</li><li>Total Fat: 0.5 g</li><li>Protein: 3.4 g</li><li>Sodium: 480 mg</li><li>Fiber: 1.1 g</li></ul>

Directions:

1. Add the starter and all bread ingredients to the bread machine pan.
2. Select the dough cycle on the machine.
3. Once the cycle is complete, preheat your oven to 350°F (175°C).
4. If the dough is sticky, incorporate more flour as needed.
5. Shape the dough on a baking sheet or place it into a loaf pan.
6. Bake for 35-40 minutes until golden brown.
7. Allow the bread to cool before slicing.

Italian Bread

	Ingredients	Nutrition
Pound Loaf	<ul><li>1¼ tablespoon of light brown sugar</li><li>4 cups all-purpose flour, unbleached</li><li>1½ teaspoons of salt</li><li>1 1/3 cups + 1¼ tablespoon warm water</li><li>1 package active dry yeast</li><li>1½ teaspoons of olive oil</li><li>1 egg</li><li>2 tablespoons cornmeal</li></ul>	<ul><li>Calories: 160</li><li>Carbohydrates: 1.6 g</li><li>Total Fat: 0.9 g</li><li>Cholesterol: 9 mg</li><li>Protein: 3.1 g</li><li>Fiber: 1 g</li><li>Sugars: 1 g</li><li>Sodium: 360 mg</li><li>Potassium: 39 mg</li></ul>

Directions:

1. Add flour, brown sugar, warm water, salt, olive oil, and yeast into the bread machine. Select the dough cycle and press start.

2. Once the cycle is complete, deflate the dough and turn it onto a floured surface.

3. Shape the dough into two loaves and place them seam side down on a cornmeal-sprinkled cutting board.

4. Cover the loaves with a damp cloth and let them rise for 40 minutes until doubled.

5. Preheat the oven to 190°C (375°F).
6. Whisk water and an egg together, then brush the mixture over the loaves.
7. Cut a slit down the center of each loaf.
8. Gently shake the cutting board to ensure the loaves are not sticking, then transfer them to a baking sheet.
9. Bake for 35 minutes.

French Baguettes

	Ingredients	Nutrition
1½-Pound Loaf	<ul><li>1¼ cups warm water</li><li>3½ cups bread flour</li><li>1 teaspoon salt</li><li>1 package active dry yeast</li></ul>	<ul><li>Calories: 160</li><li>Carbohydrates: 42 g</li><li>Total Fat 0.6 g</li><li>Cholesterol: 0 mg</li><li>Protein: 6 g</li><li>Fiber: 1.7 g</li><li>Sugars: 0.1 g</li><li>Sodium: 240 mg</li></ul>

Directions:

1. Add all ingredients to your bread machine.

2. Set the machine to the dough cycle and press start.

3. Once the cycle completes, remove the dough with floured hands and divide it in half on a floured surface.

4. Roll each piece into a 1½-foot long loaf resembling French bread.

5. Place each loaf on a greased baking sheet, cover with a towel, and let rise until doubled, about 1 hour.

6. Preheat the oven to 450° F.

7. Bake until the loaves are golden brown, rotating the baking sheet halfway through.

Pizza Basis

	Ingredients	Nutrition
1½-Pound Loaf	<ul><li>1 cups warm water</li><li>2 cups flour</li><li>1 cup Semolina flour</li><li>½ teaspoon sugar</li><li>2½ teaspoons salt</li><li>1 teaspoon olive oil</li><li>2 teaspoons yeast</li></ul>	<ul><li>Calories: 190</li><li>Total Fat: 4.4g</li><li>Saturated Fat: 0.6g</li><li>Cholesterol: 0mg</li><li>Sodium: 480g</li><li>Carbohydrates: 15.6g</li><li>Dietary Fiber: 5.9g</li><li>Total Sugars: 1.2 g</li><li>Protein: 1.9g</li></ul>

Directions:

1. Add all the ingredients to the bread machine's pan, following the manufacturer's recommended order. Choose the Dough setting.
2. Once the dough has risen, use it as the foundation for your pizza.

Cinnamon Raisin Buns

	Ingredients	Nutrition
Pound Loaf	<ul><li>½ cup milk</li><li>½ cup water</li><li>2¾ tablespoons butter</li><li>¾ teaspoon salt</li><li>3 cups flour</li><li>2¼ teaspoons yeast</li><li>3 tablespoons sugar</li><li>1 egg</li></ul>For filling<ul><li>3 tablespoons butter, melted</li><li>1 teaspoon ground cinnamon</li><li>1/3 cup sugar</li><li>1/3 cup raisins</li><li>1/3 cup chopped walnuts</li></ul>For glaze<ul><li>1 cup powdered sugar</li><li>1½ tablespoons melted butter</li><li>½ teaspoon vanilla</li><li>1½ tablespoons milk</li></ul>	<ul><li>Calories: 300</li><li>Total Fat: 9.2 g</li><li>Saturated Fat: 4.3 g</li><li>Cholesterol: 31mg</li><li>Sodium: 180 g</li><li>Carbohydrate: 53.2 g</li><li>Dietary Fiber: 1.5 g</li><li>Total Sugars: 27.7 g</li><li>Protein: 5.2 g</li></ul>

Directions:

1. Warm ½ cup of milk, water, and 2 tablespoons of butter in a saucepan until hot.

2. Add the milk mixture, salt, flour, yeast, sugar, and eggs to the bread maker's bucket in the order specified by the manufacturer. Select the Dough program and press Start.

3. When the cycle completes, remove the dough from the bread maker. Roll the dough into a large rectangle on a floured surface. Spread with softened butter.

4. Combine cinnamon and sugar, then sprinkle over the dough rectangle. Generously add raisins and/or chopped nuts.

5. Roll the dough from the long side into a log, then cut into 1½-inch pieces. Place the buns cut-side down on a greased 25x35cm baking tray.

6. Cover and let rise in a warm place until nearly doubled in size, about 30 minutes.

7. Preheat the oven to 375°F. Mix powdered sugar, 1¼ tablespoons melted butter, vanilla, and 1¼ tablespoons milk to make thick icing, and set aside.

8. Place the dough in the oven and bake until golden brown. Brush with glaze when ready.

Syrian Bread

	Ingredients	Nutrition
PoundLo af	<ul><li>2 tablespoons vegetable oil</li><li>1 cup of water</li><li>1½ teaspoon salt</li><li>½ teaspoon white sugar</li><li>1½ teaspoons active dry yeast</li><li>3 cups all-purpose flour</li></ul>	<ul><li>Calories: 168</li><li>Carbohydrates: 36 g</li><li>Total Fat 5 g</li><li>Protein: 5 g</li><li>Fiber: 1 g</li><li>Sugar: 0 g</li><li>Sodium: 360 mg</li><li>Potassium: 66 mg</li></ul>

Directions:

1. Add all ingredients into your bread machine pan.
2. Set the machine to the dough cycle and press start.
3. Preheat the oven to 475°F.
4. Once the dough is ready, turn it onto a lightly floured surface.
5. Cut the dough into eight equal pieces and shape them into rounds.
6. Cover the rounds with a damp cloth and let them rest for a few minutes.
7. Roll each round into a flat thin circle about 1½ inches in diameter.
8. Bake on preheated baking sheets until golden brown and puffed.

Italian Pie Calzone

	Ingredients	Nutrition
1½-Pound Loaf	<ul><li>1¼ cups water</li><li>1½ teaspoon salt</li><li>3 cups flour</li><li>1 teaspoon milk powder</li><li>1½ tablespoons sugar</li><li>2 teaspoons yeast</li><li>¾ cup tomato sauce for pizza</li><li>1¼ cups grated mozzarella</li><li>2 tablespoons butter, melted</li></ul>	<ul><li>Calories: 247</li><li>Total Fat: 9.2 g</li><li>Saturated Fat: 3.5 g</li><li>Cholesterol: 22 mg</li><li>Sodium: 590 g</li><li>Carbohydrates: 30 g</li><li>Dietary Fiber: 1.5 g</li><li>Sugars: 2.1½ g</li><li>Protein: 10 g</li></ul>

Directions:

1. Place the water, salt, bread flour, dry milk, sugar, and yeast into the bread maker's bucket, following the manufacturer's order. Select the Dough setting.

2. Once the cycle is complete, roll the dough out on a lightly floured surface into a 45 x 25 cm rectangle. Place it on a lightly greased baking tray.

3. Spoon the pizza sauce in a strip along the center of the dough and sprinkle with mozzarella cheese.

4. Make diagonal cuts 1½ cm apart on both sides, leaving a 1½ cm gap from the filling.

5. Cross the dough strips over the filling, moistening with water as needed. Brush with melted butter.

6. Bake at 360°F for 35 to 45 minutes.

International Bread

German Pumpernickel Bread

	Ingredients	Nutrition
2-Pound Loaf	<ul><li>1½ tablespoons vegetable oil</li><li>1½ cups warm water</li><li>3 tablespoons cocoa</li><li>1/3 cup molasses</li><li>1½ teaspoons salt</li><li>1¼ tablespoon caraway seeds</li><li>1 cup rye flour</li><li>1½ cups of bread flour</li><li>1½ tablespoons wheat gluten</li><li>1 cup whole wheat flour</li><li>2½ teaspoons bread machine yeast</li></ul>	<ul><li>Calories: 185</li><li>Carbohydrates: 22.4 g</li><li>Total Fat 2.3 g</li><li>Cholesterol: 0 mg</li><li>Protein: 3 g</li><li>Sodium: 360 mg</li></ul>

Directions:

1. Load all ingredients into your bread machine.
2. Choose the basic cycle from the machine's menu.
3. Press the start button to begin the baking process.
4. Once the baking is completed, transfer the bread to a cooling rack.

European Black Bread

	Ingredients	Nutrition
Pound Loaf	<ul><li>1 cup of water</li><li>¾ teaspoon cider vinegar</li><li>½ cup rye flour</li><li>1½ cups flour</li><li>1¼ tablespoon margarine</li><li>¼ cup of oat bran</li><li>1 teaspoon salt</li><li>1½ tablespoons sugar</li><li>1 teaspoon dried onion flakes</li><li>1 teaspoon caraway seed</li><li>1 teaspoon yeast</li><li>2 tablespoons unsweetened cocoa</li></ul>	<ul><li>Calories: 190</li><li>Carbohydrates: 22 g</li><li>Total fat: 1.7 g</li><li>Cholesterol: 0 mg</li><li>Protein: 3 g</li><li>Sugar: 2 g</li><li>Sodium: 247 mg</li></ul>

Directions:

1. Load your bread machine with all the necessary ingredients.
2. Select the basic setting from your machine's menu.
3. Press the start button to begin the bread-making process.
4. Once the baking is complete, transfer the bread to a cooling rack to cool.

Portuguese Sweet Bread

	Ingredients	Nutrition
Pound Loaf	<ul><li>1 egg beaten</li><li>1 cup milk</li><li>1/3 cup sugar</li><li>2 tablespoons margarine</li><li>3 cups bread flour</li><li>¾ teaspoon salt</li><li>2½ teaspoons active dry yeast</li></ul>	<ul><li>Calories: 180</li><li>Carbohydrates: 24 g</li><li>Total Fat: 11 ½ g</li><li>Cholesterol: 1 mg</li><li>Protein: 3 g</li><li>Fiber: 0 g</li><li>Sugars: 4 g</li><li>Sodium: 180 mg</li></ul>

Directions:

1. Add all ingredients into the bread machine.
2. Choose the sweet bread setting and press start.
3. Once the bread is done, transfer it to a cooling rack to cool.

Ethiopian Milk and Honey

	Ingredients	Nutrition
Pound Loaf	<ul><li>3 tablespoons honey</li><li>1 cup + 1¼ tablespoon milk</li><li>3 cups bread flour</li><li>3 tablespoons melted butter</li><li>2 teaspoons active dry yeast</li><li>1½ teaspoon salt</li></ul>	<ul><li>Calories: 191</li><li>Carbohydrates: 1 g</li><li>Total Fat 3.1 g</li><li>Cholesterol: 0 mg</li><li>Protein: 2.4 g</li><li>Fiber: 0.6 g</li><li>Sugars: 3.3 g</li><li>Sodium: 362 mg</li></ul>

Directions:

1. Place all ingredients into the bread machine pan.
2. Set the machine to the white bread or basic setting with a medium crust.
3. Press the start button to begin the baking process.
4. Once the bread is baked, remove it from the machine.
5. Allow the bread to cool on a wire rack.
6. Slice the bread when it is completely cooled and serve.

Fiji Sweet Potato Bread

	Ingredients	Nutrition
Pound Loaf	<ul><li>1 teaspoon vanilla extract</li><li>½ cup of warm water</li><li>4 cups flour</li><li>1 cup sweet mashed potatoes</li><li>2 tablespoons softened butter</li><li>½ teaspoon cinnamon</li><li>1½ teaspoons salt</li><li>1/3 cup brown sugar</li><li>2 tablespoons powdered milk</li><li>2 teaspoons yeast</li></ul>	<ul><li>Calories: 181</li><li>Carbohydrates: 21 g</li><li>Fat: 5 g</li><li>Protein: 4 g</li><li>Fiber: 1 g</li><li>Sugar 3 g</li><li>Sodium: 360 mg</li></ul>

Directions:

1. Place all the ingredients in your bread machine pan.
2. Select the white bread setting and choose your preferred crust option.
3. Press the start button to begin the baking process.
4. Once the bread is finished, transfer it to wire racks to cool before slicing.

Gluten-Free

Rosemary Bread

	Ingredients	Nutrition
1½-Pound Loaf	<ul><li>1 ¼ cups warm water</li><li>¼ cup olive oil</li><li>2 egg whites</li><li>1¼ tablespoon apple cider vinegar</li><li>½ teaspoon baking powder</li><li>2 teaspoons dry active yeast</li><li>2 tablespoons granulated sugar</li><li>½ teaspoon Italian seasoning</li><li>¼ teaspoon ground black pepper</li><li>1¼ teaspoons dried rosemary</li><li>2 cups gluten-free almond flour / or any other gluten-free flour, leveled</li><li>1 cup tapioca/potato starch, leveled</li><li>2 teaspoons Xanthan Gum</li><li>1 teaspoon salt</li></ul>	<ul><li>Calories: 184</li><li>Total fat: 3 g</li><li>Protein:6g</li><li>Cholesterol: 5 mg</li><li>Sodium: 240 mg</li><li>Fiber: 1 g</li><li>Carbohydrates: 24 g</li></ul>

Directions:

1. According to your bread machine's manufacturer instructions, put all the ingredients into the bread machine's greased pan.
2. Select the basic cycle and choose either medium or light crust. Press start to begin baking the bread.
3. During the last kneading cycle, check the dough. It should be wet but thick, not like traditional bread dough. If it's too wet, add more flour one tablespoon at a time until it becomes slightly firm.
4. When the cycle is finished and the machine turns off, remove the baked bread from the pan and allow it to cool on a wire rack.

Flax and Sunflower Seeds Bread

	Ingredients	Nutrition
Pound Loaf	<ul><li>1¼ cups warm water</li><li>¼ cup olive oil</li><li>2 egg whites</li><li>1¼ tablespoon apple cider vinegar</li><li>½ teaspoon baking powder</li><li>2 teaspoons dry active yeast</li><li>2 tablespoons granulated sugar</li><li>2 cups gluten-free almond flour / or any other gluten-free flour, leveled</li><li>1 cup tapioca/potato starch, leveled</li><li>2 teaspoons Xanthan Gum</li><li>1 teaspoon salt</li><li>½ cup flax seeds</li><li>½ cup sunflower seeds</li></ul>	<ul><li>Calories: 195</li><li>Total fat: 2 g</li><li>Cholesterol: 5 mg</li><li>Sodium: 240 mg</li><li>Carbohydrates: 21 g</li><li>Fiber: 2 g</li><li>Protein: 4 g</li></ul>

Directions:

1. Place all the ingredients except sunflower seeds into the bread machine's greased pan.
2. Select the basic cycle and choose either medium or light crust color. Press start to begin baking the bread.
3. During the last kneading cycle, check the dough. It should be wet but thick, not like traditional bread dough. If it's too wet, add more flour one tablespoon at a time until it is slightly firm.
4. Add the sunflower seeds 5 minutes before the kneading cycle ends.
5. Once the baking cycle is complete, remove the baked bread from the pan and allow it to cool on a wire rack.

Italian Parmesan Cheese Bread

	Ingredients	Nutrition
2 Pound Loaf	<ul><li>1¼ cups warm water</li><li>¼ cup olive oil</li><li>2 egg whites</li><li>1¼ tablespoon apple cider vinegar</li><li>½ teaspoon baking powder</li><li>2 teaspoons dry active yeast</li><li>2 tablespoons granulated sugar</li><li>2 cups gluten-free almond flour / or any other gluten-free flour, leveled</li><li>1 cup tapioca/potato starch, leveled</li><li>2 teaspoons Xanthan Gum</li><li>¼ cup grated Parmesan cheese</li><li>1 teaspoon salt</li><li>1 teaspoon Italian seasoning</li><li>1 teaspoon garlic powder</li></ul>	<ul><li>Calories: 190</li><li>Total fat: 2 g</li><li>Cholesterol: 2 mg</li><li>Sodium: 240 mg</li><li>Carbohydrates: 15 g</li><li>Fiber: 1 g</li><li>Protein: 2 g</li></ul>

Directions:

1. Put all the ingredients into the bread machine's greased pan. Select the basic cycle. Choose the crust color—either medium or light—and press start to bake the bread.

2. Check the dough during the final kneading cycle. It should not be as thick as typical bread dough but rather wet. If the dough is too wet, add extra flour, one tablespoon at a time, until it becomes somewhat firm.

3. When the cycle is finished and your machine turns off, remove the baked bread from the pan and cool it on a wire rack.

Cheese & Herb Bread

Ingredients	Nutrition
<ul><li>1¼ cups warm water</li><li>¼ cup olive oil</li><li>2 egg whites</li><li>1¼ tablespoon apple cider vinegar</li><li>½ teaspoon baking powder</li><li>2 teaspoons dry active yeast</li><li>2 tablespoons granulated sugar</li><li>2 cups gluten-free almond flour / or any other gluten-free flour, leveled</li><li>1 cup Tapioca/potato starch, leveled</li><li>2 teaspoons Xanthan Gum</li><li>1 teaspoon salt</li><li>2 tablespoons grated Parmesan cheese</li><li>1 teaspoon dried marjoram</li><li>¾ teaspoon dried basil</li><li>¾ teaspoon dried oregano</li></ul>	<ul><li>Calories: 231</li><li>Total fat: 3 g</li><li>Cholesterol: 5 mg</li><li>Sodium: 245 mg</li><li>Carbohydrates: 19 g</li><li>Fiber: 1 g</li><li>Protein: 4 g</li></ul>

Directions:

1. Put all the ingredients into the bread machine's greased pan. Select the basic cycle. Choose the crust color—either medium or light—and press start to bake the bread.

2. During the last kneading cycle, check the dough. It should be wet but thick, not like traditional bread dough. If the dough is too wet, add more flour, one tablespoon at a time, until the dough is slightly firm.

3. When the cycle is finished and the machine turns off, remove the baked bread from the pan and cool it on a wire rack.

Cinnamon Raisin Bread

	Ingredients	Nutrition
2-Pound Loaf	<ul><li>1¼ cups warm water</li><li>¼ cup olive oil</li><li>2 tablespoons honey</li><li>2 egg whites</li><li>1¼ tablespoon apple cider vinegar</li><li>½ teaspoon baking powder</li><li>2 teaspoons dry active yeast</li><li>2 tablespoons granulated sugar</li><li>2 cups gluten-free almond flour / or any other gluten-free flour, leveled</li><li>1 cup Tapioca/potato starch, leveled</li><li>2 teaspoons Xanthan Gum</li><li>1 teaspoon salt</li><li>1 teaspoon ground cinnamon</li><li>1 cup raisins</li></ul>	<ul><li>Calories: 219</li><li>Fat: 1 g</li><li>Cholesterol: 2 mg</li><li>Sodium: 240 mg</li><li>Carbohydrates: 22 g</li></ul>

Directions:

1. Place all the ingredients, excluding the raisins, into the greased pan of your bread maker. Select the basic cycle. Choose the crust color, either medium or light, and press start to begin baking the bread.

2. During the last kneading cycle, check the dough. It should be wet but thick, not like traditional bread dough. If the dough is too wet, add more flour, one tablespoon at a time, until the dough is slightly firm.

3. Add the raisins 5 minutes before the kneading cycle ends.

4. Once the cycle is complete and the machine turns off, remove the baked bread from the pan and cool it on a wire rack.

Keto Bread

Bulgur Bread

	Ingredients	Nutrition
1½-Pound Loaf	<ul><li>½ cup bulgur</li><li>1/3 cup boiling water</li><li>1 egg</li><li>1 cup water</li><li>1¼ tablespoon butter</li><li>1½ tablespoons milk powder</li><li>1¼ tablespoon sugar</li><li>2 teaspoons salt</li><li>3¼ cup flour</li><li>1 teaspoon dried yeast</li></ul>	<ul><li>Calories: 250</li><li>Carbohydrates: 3 g</li><li>Fats: 3 g</li><li>Protein: 1½ g</li><li>Sodium: 480 mg</li><li>Fiber: 1.2 g</li></ul>

Directions:

1. Pour boiling water over the bulgur in a small bowl or container, then cover it with a lid. Let it stand for 30 minutes.

2. For best results, cut the butter into small cubes.

3. In a measuring cup or container, stir the egg with water until the total volume reaches 300 ml.

4. Place all the ingredients into the bread maker in the order specified in your bread maker's instructions. Select the basic mode with a medium crust and start baking.

Almond Meal Bread

	Ingredients	Nutrition
Pound Loaf	• 4 eggs, pasteurized • ¼ cup melted coconut oil • 1¼ tablespoon apple cider vinegar • 2¼ cups almond meal • 1 teaspoon baking soda • ¼ cup ground flaxseed meal • 1 teaspoon onion powder • 1¼ tablespoon minced garlic • 1 teaspoon of sea salt • 1 teaspoon chopped sage leaves • 1 teaspoon fresh thyme • 1 teaspoon chopped rosemary leaves	• Calories: 190 • Sodium: 240 mg • Fat: 2 g • Protein: 4 g • Carbohydrates: 2.1 g • Fiber: 2 g • Net Carbohydrates: 0.3 g

Directions:

1. Gather all the ingredients for the bread and plug in the bread machine with a 2-pound capacity.

2. In a large bowl, crack the eggs and beat them with the coconut oil and vinegar until well blended.

3. In another large bowl, place the almond meal, add the remaining dry ingredients, and stir until well mixed.

4. Pour the egg mixture into the bread machine pan, top with the flour mixture, close the lid, select the "basic/white" cycle or "low-carb" setting, and adjust the baking time using the up/down arrow button on your bread machine; typically, this will take 3 to 4 hours.

5. If available, press the crust button to select a light crust, then press the "start/stop" button to begin the bread machine.

6. When the bread machine completes the cycle and beeps, open the lid, remove the bread pan, and carefully lift out the bread.

7. Allow the bread to cool slightly on a wire rack for about 1 hour, then slice it into ten pieces and serve.

Italian Blue Cheese Bread

	Ingredients	Nutrition
1½-Pound Loaf	<ul><li>1 teaspoon dry yeast</li><li>2½ cups almond flour</li><li>1½ teaspoon salt</li><li>1¼ tablespoon sugar</li><li>1¼ tablespoon olive oil</li><li>½ cup blue cheese</li><li>1 cup water</li></ul>	<ul><li>Calories: 190</li><li>Carbohydrates 5 g</li><li>Fats 4.6 g</li><li>Protein: 6 g</li><li>Fiber: 1.5 g</li><li>Sodium: 360 mg</li></ul>

Directions:

1. Mix all the necessary ingredients for the bread and load them into the bread machine pan.

2. Start the baking cycle using the standard mode setting.

3. Once the bread machine completes its cycle, carefully remove the baked bread from the pan and allow it to cool on a wire rack.

Macadamia Nut Bread

	Ingredients	Nutrition
½-Pound Loaf	• 1 cup / 135 grams macadamia nuts • 5 eggs, pasteurized • 1 cup water • ½ teaspoon apple cider vinegar • ½ cup / 30 grams coconut flour • ½ teaspoon baking soda	• Calories: 165 • Sodium: 20 mg • Fat: 1.3 g • Protein: 5.6 g • Carbohydrates: 3.9 g • Fiber: 3 g • Net Carbohydrates: 0.9 g

Directions:

1. Gather all the bread ingredients and prepare the bread machine designed for a 1-pound loaf.

2. Add nuts to a blender and pulse for 2 to 3 minutes until they reach a butter-like consistency. Then add eggs and vinegar and blend until the mixture is smooth.

3. Mix in the flour and baking soda thoroughly. Transfer the batter to the bread machine's pan, close the lid, select the "basic/white" cycle or the "low-carb" option, and use the up/down arrows to set the baking time according to your machine's specifications; typically, this will take about 3 to 4 hours.

4. If your machine allows, select a light crust by pressing the crust button, then start the bread machine by pressing the "start/stop" button.

5. When the bread machine beeps, open the lid, remove the bread pan, and carefully lift out the bread. Allow the bread to cool on a wire rack for 1 hour, then slice it into eight pieces and serve.

Cheesy Garlic Bread

	Ingredients	Nutrition
2 Pound Loaf	• 5 eggs, pasteurized • 1 cup water • 2 cups / 10 grams almond flour • ½ teaspoon Xanthan gum • 1 teaspoon garlic powder • 1 teaspoon salt • 1 teaspoon parsley • 1 teaspoon Italian seasoning • 1 teaspoon dried oregano • 1 stick of butter, grass-fed, unsalted, melted • 1 cup grated mozzarella cheese • 2 tablespoons ricotta cheese • 1 cup / 235 grams grated cheddar cheese • 1/3 cup / 30 grams grated parmesan cheese For the Topping: • ½ stick of butter, grass-fed, unsalted, melted • 1 teaspoon garlic powder	• Calories: 245 • Fat: 1.5 g • Sodium: 400 mg • Protein: 7.2 g • Carbohydrates: 3 g • Fiber: 1.6 g • Net Carbohydrates: 1.4 g

Directions:

1. After assembling all the bread ingredients, insert them into the 2-pound bread machine.

2. Crack the eggs into a large bowl and whisk to combine.

3. In a separate large bowl, whisk together the flour, Xanthan gum, and all the cheeses until well blended.

4. In a medium bowl, melt the butter, add all the seasonings, and stir until mixed.

5. Pour the egg mixture into the bread machine pan, top with the seasoning mixture and flour mixture, then close the lid. Select the "basic" or "white" cycle, or choose the "low-carb" setting. Adjust the baking time using the up/down arrow button on your bread machine; typically, it will take 3 to 4 hours.

6. Press the crust button to select a light crust if available, then press the "start/stop" button to start the bread machine.

7. When the bread machine beeps, open the lid, remove the bread pan, and lift out the bread.

8. Prepare the topping by mixing melted butter and garlic powder, then brush the mixture on top of the bread.

9. Allow the bread to cool on a wire rack for an hour, then slice it into sixteen pieces and serve.

Keto Almond Pumpkin Quick Bread

	Ingredients	Nutrition
1½-Pound Loaf	<ul><li>1/3 cup vegetable oil</li><li>½ cup water</li><li>3 large eggs</li><li>1 ½ cups pumpkin puree, canned</li><li>1 cup granulated sugar</li><li>1½ teaspoons baking powder</li><li>½ teaspoon baking soda</li><li>¼ teaspoon salt</li><li>¾ teaspoon ground cinnamon</li><li>¼ teaspoon ground nutmeg</li><li>¼ teaspoon ground ginger</li><li>3 cups almond flour</li><li>½ cup chopped pecans</li></ul>	<ul><li>Calories: 245</li><li>Sodium: 70 mg</li><li>Fat: 1.5 g</li><li>Protein: 7.2 g</li><li>Carbohydrates: 3 g</li><li>Fiber: 1.6 g</li><li>Net Carbohydrates: 1.4 g</li></ul>

Directions:

1. Spray the pan in your bread maker with cooking spray.

2. Combine all the wet ingredients in a bowl and stir to mix. Add all the dry ingredients (except the pecans) and mix well.

3. After adding the batter to the pan, place the pan inside the bread maker. Close the lid securely.

4. Press START, select the QUICK BREAD cycle, and start the bread maker.

5. When the bread machine signals, open the lid and add the chopped pecans. Close the lid and press START to resume the cycle.

6. Once the cycle is complete, remove the loaf from the pan and place it on a cooling rack.

7. Slice and serve with your favorite keto soup.

Keto Basil Parmesan Slices

	Ingredients	Nutrition
1½-Pound Loaf	<ul><li>1 cup water</li><li>½ cup parmesan cheese, grated</li><li>3 tablespoons sugar</li><li>1¼ tablespoon dried basil</li><li>1½ tablespoons olive oil</li><li>1 teaspoon salt</li><li>3 cups almond flour</li><li>2 teaspoons active dry yeast</li></ul>	<ul><li>Calories: 245</li><li>Sodium: 240 mg</li><li>Fat: 1.5 g</li><li>Protein: 7.2 g</li><li>Carbohydrates: 3 g</li><li>Fiber: 1.6 g</li><li>Net Carbohydrates: 1.4 g</li></ul>

Directions:

1. As directed by the ingredients list, add all of the ingredients to the pan of your bread maker.

2. Select the BASIC cycle on your bread maker and press START after closing the cover.

3. Place the loaf on a cooling rack once the cycle is finished.

4. Slice the loaf in half and serve as an accompaniment to your main meal or soup.

Keto Onion Bread

	Ingredients	Nutrition
2-Pound Loaf	<ul><li>1½ cups water</li><li>2 tablespoons + 2 teaspoons butter, unsalted</li><li>1½ teaspoons salt</li><li>1¼ tablespoon + 1 teaspoon sugar</li><li>2 tablespoons + 2 teaspoons non-fat dry milk</li><li>4 cups almond flour</li><li>2 teaspoons active dry yeast</li><li>4 tablespoons dry onion soup mix</li></ul>	<ul><li>Calories: 245</li><li>Sodium: 360 mg</li><li>Fat: 1.5 g</li><li>Protein: 7.2 g</li><li>Carbs: 3 g</li><li>Fiber: 1.6 g</li></ul>

Directions:

1. As directed in the list above, add all ingredients to the bread machine pan except for the dry onion soup mix.

2. Close the lid. Select the BASIC cycle on your bread maker and press START.

3. After thirty to forty minutes, your machine will signal. This is the time to add any desired fruit, nuts, or seasoning to your dough. Add the dry onion soup mix to the bread machine and pause the cycle.

4. Resume the cycle by pressing the START button.

5. Once the loaf is done, transfer it to a cooling rack.

6. Slice and serve as a side dish for soup, or with butter or cream cheese.

Keto Sundried Tomato Quick Bread

	Ingredients	Nutrition
1½-Pound Loaf	<ul><li>2¼ cups almond flour</li><li>½ water</li><li>1¼ tablespoon baking powder</li><li>1 teaspoon kosher salt</li><li>3 large eggs</li><li>1½ cups buttermilk</li><li>6 tablespoons canola oil</li><li>1¼ tablespoon dried basil</li><li>1 cup sundried tomato roughly chopped</li></ul>	<ul><li>Calories: 253</li><li>Sodium: 230 mg</li><li>Fat: 1.5 g</li><li>Protein: 7.2 g</li><li>Carbohydrates: 3 g</li><li>Fiber: 1.6 g</li><li>Net Carbohydrates: 1.4 g</li></ul>

Directions:

1. As directed by the above list, add all ingredients—aside from the dry onion soup mix to the bread machine pan.
2. Shut the cover. On your bread maker, select the BASIC cycle and hit START.
3. After thirty to forty minutes, your system will ping. This is the time to include any desired fruit, nut, or seasoning into your dough. Put the dry onion soup mix in your bread machine and pause it.
4. Restart the cycle by pressing the START button.
5. When the loaf is done, move it to a cooling rack.
6. Cut into slices and serve as a side dish for soup, or with butter or cream cheese.

Keto Cheddar Bacon and Chive Bread

	Ingredients	Nutrition
1½-Pound Loaf	<ul><li>2¼ cups almond flour</li><li>½ water</li><li>1¼ tablespoon baking powder</li><li>1 teaspoon kosher salt</li><li>3 large eggs</li><li>1½ cups buttermilk</li><li>6 tablespoons canola oil</li><li>3 tablespoons finely chopped chives</li><li>1 cup shredded cheddar sharp cheese</li><li>6 strips bacon cook and crumbled</li></ul>	<ul><li>Calories: 242</li><li>Sodium: 270 mg</li><li>Fat: 1.5 g</li><li>Protein: 7.2 g</li><li>Carbohydrates: 3 g</li><li>Fiber: 1.6 g</li><li>Net Carbohydrates: 1.4 g</li></ul>

Directions:

1. Except for the bacon, add all the ingredients to the bread maker pan.

2. Close the lid. Select the QUICK BREAD setting on your bread maker and press START.

3. Wait for the signal indicating to add the fruit and nuts. Add the bacon, pause the machine, open the lid, and then resume by pressing START after closing the lid again.

4. Once the cycle is complete, transfer the loaf to a wire cooling rack.

5. Slice and serve.

Keto Tortilla Wraps

	Ingredients	Nutrition
Pound Loaf	• 1 cup golden flaxseed meal • 2 tablespoons coconut flour • ½ teaspoon Xanthan gum • ½ teaspoon salt • 1¼ tablespoon butter • 1 cup warm water	• Calories: 235 • Sodium: 130 mg • Fat: 1.5 g • Protein: 7.2 g • Carbohydrates: 3 g • Fiber: 1.6 g • Net Carbohydrates: 1.4 g

Directions:

1. Place all the ingredients into your bread machine and close the lid.

2. Choose the DOUGH cycle and press START.

3. After the cycle completes, take the dough out and place it on a lightly floured surface.

4. Cut the dough into equal pieces and roll each piece into a thin layer.

5. Heat a skillet over low heat and cook each tortilla for 1-2 minutes on each side.

6. Remove from the skillet and keep them covered with a towel to keep them soft.

7. Enjoy the tortillas with your preferred filling.

Ricotta Chive Bread

	Ingredients	Nutrition
Pound Loaf	<ul><li>1 cup lukewarm water</li><li>1/3 cup whole or part-skim ricotta cheese</li><li>1½ teaspoons salt</li><li>1¼ tablespoon granulated sugar</li><li>3 cups bread flour</li><li>½ cup chopped chives</li><li>2½ teaspoons instant yeast</li></ul>	<ul><li>Calories:190</li><li>Sodium: 370 mg</li><li>Total Fat: 0 g</li><li>Cholesterol: 2 mg</li><li>Sodium: 360 mg</li><li>Carbohydrates: 17 g</li><li>Fiber: 1 g</li><li>Protein: 3 g</li></ul>

Directions:

1. Place all the ingredients, except the dried fruit, into the bread machine pan.

2. Select the basic bread setting and choose either a light or medium crust.

Pumpkin Pecan Bread

	Ingredients	Nutrition
Pound Loaf	<ul><li>½ cup milk</li><li>½ cup canned pumpkin</li><li>1 egg</li><li>2 tablespoons margarine or butter, cut up</li><li>3 cups bread flour</li><li>3 tablespoons packed brown sugar</li><li>¾ teaspoon salt</li><li>¼ teaspoon ground nutmeg</li><li>¼ teaspoon ground ginger</li><li>1½ teaspoons ground cloves</li><li>1 teaspoon active dry yeast or bread machine yeast</li><li>¾ cup coarsely chopped pecans</li></ul>	<ul><li>Calories: 185</li><li>Fat: 6 g</li><li>Cholesterol: 1 mg</li><li>Sodium: 186 mg</li><li>Carbohydrates: 23 g</li><li>Fiber: 4 g</li><li>Protein: 4 g</li></ul>

Directions:

1. Fill the bread machine pan with all the ingredients.
2. Choose the basic cycle.
3. Remove the baked bread from the pan and allow it to cool on a wire rack once the cycle is complete and the machine shuts off.

Red Hot Cinnamon

	Ingredients	Nutrition
Pound Loaf	<ul><li>¼ cup lukewarm water</li><li>½ cup lukewarm milk</li><li>¼ cup softened butter</li><li>2¼ teaspoons instant yeast</li><li>1¼ teaspoons salt</li><li>¼ cup sugar</li><li>1 teaspoon vanilla</li><li>1 large egg, lightly beaten</li><li>3 cups all-purpose flour</li><li>½ cup Cinnamon Red Hot candies</li></ul>	<ul><li>Calories: 180</li><li>Total Fat: 6.9 g</li><li>Cholesterol: 18 mg</li><li>Sodium: 367 mg</li><li>Carbohydrates: 30 g</li><li>Fiber: 1 g</li><li>Protein: 4.6 g</li></ul>

Directions:

1. Except for the candy, add all ingredients to the bread machine pan.
2. Select the dough setting.
3. Once the cycle is over, place the dough in a bowl, cover it, and allow it to rise for forty-five to sixty minutes.
4. Shape the dough into a rectangular shape by gently pressing it down.
5. Knead in the cinnamon candies one third at a time.
6. Shape the dough into a loaf and place it in a loaf pan lined with parchment paper or oiled.

7. Let the dough rise again in the pan, loosely covered with lightly oiled plastic wrap, for 40 to 50 minutes.

8. Preheat the oven to 350 degrees Fahrenheit.

9. Bake for thirty to forty minutes. Remove from the pan and let cool on a wire rack before slicing.

Cheddar Olive Loaf

	Ingredients	Nutrition
Pound Loaf	<ul><li>1 cup water room temperature</li><li>4 teaspoons sugar</li><li>¾ teaspoon salt</li><li>1¼ cups shredded sharp cheddar cheese</li><li>3 cups bread flour</li><li>2 teaspoons active dry yeast</li><li>¾ cup pimiento olives, drained and sliced</li></ul>	<ul><li>Calories: 167</li><li>Total Fat: 4 g (2 g sat. fat)</li><li>Cholesterol: 9 mg</li><li>Sodium: 299 mg</li><li>Carbohydrates: 19 g</li><li>Fiber: 1 g</li><li>Protein: 5 g</li></ul>

Directions:

1. Add all ingredients to the machine pan except the olives.

2. Choose the default bread setting.

3. Add the olives just before the second kneading cycle.

4. Continue baking until the bread machine finishes its cycle.

Wild Rice Cranberry

	Ingredients	Nutrition
1½-Pound Loaf	<ul><li>1¼ cups water</li><li>¼ cup skim milk powder</li><li>1¼ teaspoons salt</li><li>2 tablespoons liquid honey</li><li>1¼ tablespoon extra-virgin olive oil</li><li>3 cup all-purpose flour</li><li>¾ cup cooked wild rice</li><li>¼ cup pine nuts</li><li>¾teaspoons celery seeds</li><li>1½ teaspoons freshly ground black pepper</li><li>1 teaspoon bread machine or instant yeast</li><li>2⁄3 cup dried cranberries</li></ul>	<ul><li>Calories: 220</li><li>Total Fat: 7.1 g</li><li>Cholesterol: 5 mg</li><li>Sodium: 322 mg</li><li>Carbohydrates: 33 g</li><li>Fiber. 1 g</li><li>Protein: 6.7 g</li></ul>

Directions:

1. Except for the cranberries, add all the ingredients to the bread machine pan.
2. Place the pan inside the chamber of the bread machine.
3. Choose the default bread setting.
4. Add the cranberries when the machine indicates to add ingredients.

Cheese Cauliflower Broccoli

	Ingredients	Nutrition
Pound Loaf	<ul><li>¼ cup water</li><li>4 tablespoons oil</li><li>1 egg white</li><li>1 teaspoon lemon juice</li><li>2/3 cup grated cheddar cheese</li><li>3 tablespoons green onion</li><li>½ cup broccoli, chopped</li><li>½ cup cauliflower, chopped</li><li>½ teaspoon lemon-pepper seasoning</li><li>2 cups bread flour</li><li>1 teaspoon regular or quick-rising yeast</li></ul>	<ul><li>Calories: 195</li><li>Total Fat: 7.4 g</li><li>Cholesterol: 1½ mg</li><li>Sodium: 56 mg</li><li>Carbohydrates: 17 g</li><li>Protein: 4.9 g</li></ul>

Directions:

1. Fill the machine pan with all the ingredients.
2. Choose the basic bread setting.
3. Take out the baked bread from the pan and let it cool on a wire rack once the cycle is complete and the machine shuts off.

Orange Cappuccino Bread Preparation

	Ingredients	Nutrition
Pound Loaf	<ul><li>1 cup water</li><li>1¼ tablespoon instant coffee granules</li><li>2 tablespoons butter or margarine, softened</li><li>1 teaspoon grated orange peel</li><li>3 cups bread flour</li><li>2 tablespoons dry milk</li><li>¼ cup sugar</li><li>1¼ teaspoons salt</li><li>2¼ teaspoons bread machine or quick active dry yeast</li></ul>	<ul><li>Calories: 172</li><li>Total Fat: 2 g</li><li>Cholesterol: 5 mg</li><li>Sodium: 300 mg</li><li>Carbohydrates: 31 g</li><li>Fiber: 1 g</li><li>Protein: 4 g</li></ul>

Directions:

1. Fill the machine pan with all the ingredients.
2. Choose the default bread setting.

Celery Bread

	Ingredients	Nutrition
Poun d Loaf	<ul><li>1 cup(5oz.) can cream of celery soup</li><li>3 tablespoons low-fat milk, heated</li><li>1¼ tablespoon vegetable oil</li><li>1¼ teaspoons celery, garlic, or onion salt</li><li>¾ cup celery, fresh/sliced thin</li><li>1¼ tablespoon celery leaves, fresh, chopped - optional</li><li>1 egg</li><li>3 cups bread flour</li><li>¼ teaspoon sugar</li><li>¼ teaspoon ginger</li><li>½ cup quick-cooking oats</li><li>2 tablespoons gluten</li><li>2 teaspoons celery seeds</li><li>1 package active dry yeast</li></ul>	<ul><li>Calories: 175</li><li>Total Fat: 3.6 g</li><li>Cholesterol: 55 mg</li><li>Sodium: 366 mg</li><li>Carbohydrates: 1½ g</li><li>Fiber: 0 g</li><li>Protein: 2.6 g</li></ul>

Directions:

1. Put everything into the bread machine pan.
2. Choose the basic bread setting.
3. Remove the baked bread from the pan and let it cool on a wire rack once the cycle is complete and the machine shuts off.

Anise Almond

	Ingredients	Nutrition
Pound Loaf	<ul><li>¾ cup water</li><li>1 or ¼ cup egg substitute</li><li>¼ cup butter or margarine, softened</li><li>¼ cup sugar</li><li>½ teaspoon salt</li><li>3 cups bread flour</li><li>1 teaspoon anise seed</li><li>2 teaspoons active dry yeast</li><li>½ cup almonds, chopped small</li></ul>	<ul><li>Calories: 200</li><li>Total Fat: 4 g</li><li>Cholesterol: 4 mg</li><li>Sodium: 124 mg</li><li>Carbohydrates: 7 g</li><li>Fiber: 0 g</li><li>Protein: 3 g</li></ul>

Directions:

1. Except for the almonds, add all the ingredients to the machine pan.
2. Choose the basic bread setting.
3. Add the almonds when prompted.

Variety of Flours Used

Almond Flour Bread

	Ingredients	Nutrition
Pound Loaf	<ul><li>4 egg whites</li><li>2 egg yolks</li><li>2 cups almond flour</li><li>¼ cup butter, melted</li><li>2 tablespoons psyllium husk powder</li><li>1½ tablespoons baking powder</li><li>½ teaspoon Xanthan gum</li><li>¼ teaspoon salt</li><li>½ cup + 2 tablespoons warm water</li><li>2¼ teaspoons yeast</li></ul>	<ul><li>Calories: 211</li><li>Sodium: 60 mg</li><li>Carbohydrates: 2.4 g</li><li>Protein: 4 g</li></ul>

Directions:

1. Combine all the dry ingredients (except the yeast) in a mixing bowl or dish.

2. Place all the wet ingredients in the bread machine pan.

3. Transfer all the dry ingredients from the mixing bowl into the bread machine pan.

4. Turn the machine on to its default settings.

5. Remove the bread from the bread machine pan once it's done.

6. Transfer it to a cooling rack after allowing it to cool slightly.

7. It keeps well for three months in the freezer and for four days on the counter.

Coconut Flour Bread

	Ingredients	Nutrition
1½ Pound Loaf	<ul><li>6 eggs</li><li>½ cup coconut flour</li><li>2 tablespoons psyllium husk</li><li>¼ cup olive oil</li><li>1½ teaspoon salt</li><li>1¼ tablespoon Xanthan gum</li><li>1¼ tablespoon baking powder</li><li>2¼ teaspoons yeast</li></ul>	<ul><li>Calories: 210</li><li>Sodium: 360 mg</li><li>Carbohydrates: 4 g</li><li>Protein: 7g</li><li>Fat: 15 g</li></ul>

Directions:

1. With the exception of the yeast, mix all the dry ingredients together in a small bowl or basin.

2. Place all the wet ingredients in the bread machine pan.

3. Transfer all the dry ingredients from the small mixing bowl into the bread machine pan. Add the yeast on top.

4. Turn the machine on to its default settings.

5. Remove the bread machine pan from the machine once the bread is done.

6. Transfer the bread to a cooling rack after allowing it to cool slightly.

7. It keeps well for up to three months in the freezer and for four days on the counter.

Warm Spiced Pumpkin

	Ingredients	Nutrition
1½-Pound Loaf	• 1½ cups pumpkin purée • 3 eggs, at room temperature • 1/3 cup melted butter cooled • 1 cup of sugar • 3 cups all-purpose flour • 1½ teaspoons baking powder • ¾ teaspoon ground cinnamon • ½ teaspoon baking soda • ¼ teaspoon ground nutmeg • ¼ teaspoon ground ginger • ¼ teaspoon salt • Pinch ground cloves	• Calories: 250 • Fat: 7g • Carbohydrates: 43 g • Fiber: 2 g • Sodium: 159 mg • Protein: 5 g

Directions:

1. Apply a thin layer of butter to the bread bucket.
2. Add the sugar, butter, eggs, and pumpkin.
3. Press Start after configuring the machine to the Quick/Rapid preset.

4. Allow the wet ingredients to continue mixing for approximately five minutes, or until the initial fast mixing cycle is complete.

5. Mix the flour, baking powder, cinnamon, baking soda, nutmeg, ginger, salt, and cloves well while the wet ingredients are combining.

6. At the beginning of the second quick mixing cycle, add the dry ingredients to the bucket.

7. Once the dry ingredients have combined with the wet mixture, scrape down the sides of the bucket.

8. Take the bread bucket out of the machine after the bread is done.

9. Give it five minutes to cool.

10. After removing the bread with a gentle shake, place it on a cooling rack.

Multigrain Bread

	Ingredients	Nutrition
1½-Pound Loaf	<ul><li>¾ cups of water</li><li>1 tablespoon melted butter cooled</li><li>½ tablespoon honey</li><li>½ teaspoon salt</li><li>¾ cup multigrain flour</li><li>1 1/3 cups white bread flour</li><li>1 teaspoon bread machine or active dry yeast</li></ul>	<ul><li>Calories: 160</li><li>Fat: 2 g</li><li>Carbohydrates: 27 g</li><li>Fiber: 1 g</li><li>Sodium: 205 mg</li><li>Protein: 4 g</li></ul>

Directions:

1. According to the manufacturer's recommendations, load the ingredients into the machine/device/appliance.

2. Press the Start button after programming the machine to make a basic white bread with a light or medium crust.

3. Take the bread pan/bucket out of the machine when the cycle is done.

4. Give it five minutes to cool.

5. After removing the bread with a gentle shake, place it on a cooling rack.

Whole-Wheat Seed

	Ingredients	Nutrition
1½-Pound Loaf	<ul><li>¾ cup of water, at 80°F</li><li>1¼ tablespoon honey</li><li>1 tablespoon melted butter cooled</li><li>½ teaspoon salt</li><li>2 cups whole-wheat flour</li><li>½ cup white bread flour</li><li>2 tablespoons raw sunflower seeds</li><li>1¼ tablespoon sesame seeds</li><li>teaspoon bread machine or instant yeast</li></ul>	<ul><li>Calories: 165</li><li>Sodium: 125 mg</li><li>Fat: 3 g</li><li>Carbohydrates: 39 g</li></ul>

Directions:

1. According to the manufacturer's recommendations, load the ingredients into your machine.
2. Set the machine to produce whole-grain/whole-wheat bread. Click Start and choose light or medium crust.
3. Remove the bucket from the machine after the bread is done.
4. Let it cool for five minutes.
5. After removing the bread with a gentle shake, place it on a cooling rack.

List of used literature

1. Kalinina I.V. Bread: An Encyclopedia. - M.: Publishing House "Food Industry", 2011.

2. Drobzhalova A.N. Baking Technology. - St. Petersburg: GIORD, 2005.

3. Auerman L.Ya. Baking Technology. - M.: Profession, 2005.

4. Olsen A. Bread: Over 60 World-Famous Breads. - M.: Eksmo, 2013.

5. Puchkova L.I. Laboratory Workshop on Baking Technology. - St. Petersburg: GIORD, 2004.

6. Tsyganova T.B. Baking Technology. - M.: Academy, 2008.

7. Dragovoz I.V. Bread All Year Round. - M.: Tsentrpoligraf, 2007.

8. Lurie I.S. Technological Equipment of Bakeries. - St. Petersburg: Profession, 2005.

9. Nechaev A.P. Food Chemistry. - St. Petersburg: GIORD, 2007.

10. Matveeva T.V., Belyavskaya I.G. Homemade Bread. Best Recipes. - M.: Eksmo, 2014.

11. Reinhart P. The Bread Baker's Apprentice. - Ten Speed Press, 2001.

12. Hamelman J. Bread: A Baker's Book of Techniques and Recipes. - Wiley, 2004.

13. Leader D. Bread Alone. - William Morrow Cookbooks, 1993.

14. Buehler R. Bread Science. - Ingram Pub Services, 2017.

15. Bas J.M. The Panera Bread Cookbook. - Crown Publishing Group, 2007.

16. Lion D. Homemade Bread. - M.: BBPG, 2008.

17. Reinhold R. Yeast-Free Breads. - M.: Volkhiz, 2014.

18. Gregory L. Rye and Wheat Breads. - St. Petersburg: Lenizdat, 2016.

19. Vatine A. French Buns and Breads. - M.: EKSMO, 2011.

20. Weiner D. Bread Machine. 200 Recipes. - Rostov-on-Don: Phoenix, 2013.

21. Hannah S. Bread. A Culinary Journey. - M.: Makhaon, 2021.

22. Rice D. Russian Bread. - St. Petersburg: Limbus Press, 2009.

23. Heinz P. Rye Breads for Health. - M.: Tsentrpoligraf, 2019.

24. Lakedemonian A.M. The Bread Country. - Yekaterinburg: U-Factoria, 2008.

25. Mikhailov N.I. Handbook of a Baking Technologist. - St. Petersburg: GIORD, 2005.

26. Fletcher G. Amazing Bread Machine Book. - Avery, 2003.

27. Cunningham M. The Bread Baker's Apprentice Mastering The Art. - Ten Speed Press, 2017.

28. Glazkovskaya M.A. Methods of Studying Properties of Raw Materials and Finished Products in Baking. - M.: DeLi print, 2006.

29. Lee-Sperr S. Baking Step-by-Step. - M.: Kladez-Buks, 2005.

30. Brandt M.V. Delicious Bread Traditions. - M.: EKSMO, 2010.